RAISING
AN EXPLOSIVE
CHILD

A NEW APPROACH TO DISCIPLINING AND POSITIVE
PARENTING HYPERACTIVE AND DISTRACTED CHILDREN,
LEARN EMOTIONAL CONTROL STRATEGIES TO HELP YOUR
CHILD SELF-REGULATE

HELEN PARENT

TABLE OF CONTENTS

INTRODUCTION

"The only parental expectation that matters? My child's joy"

This book provides helpful elements in dealing specifically with children with explosive disorders. While there are a variety of therapies that can help alleviate symptoms, determining the best way to manage the child's explosions at home is not straightforward, this book will provide you with all the necessary advice and offer you knowledge and resources to assist your explosive child is feeling in command and on the right track.

We also want to raise children who know how to manage their behavior, both because it is easier to live with and our job as parents. We also know how to raise those children. When we regulate our emotions, our children learn to regulate their emotions. It allows them to regulate their behavior, assuming they are connected enough with us to want to.

For parents, teachers, and families dealing with an explosive child, this practical book is a groove with suggestions, advice, and support for explosive children. It contains all of the parenting techniques you may use at home to treat your child correctly.

While you educate yourself and familiarize yourself with the disorder, you are helping your child to cope by providing them with solutions that make life seem easier.

Even if you are not changing much, simply changing the way that view a situation can prevent them from becoming triggered. It is so important for you to learn your child's triggers and how you can avoid them. You must also have a backup plan that you can implement for when the meltdowns do occur.

The most challenging aspect of raising an explosive child is managing his life. It's critical to figure out how to harness it and give him routines. If you have a kid with any explosive disorder, it is essential that you first become aware of how to manage it, its possible causes, and what encourages your child to deal with the disorder's manifestations. Attention deficit hyperactivity disorder can cause many difficulties in children and adolescents, but there are many things you can do to help.

It is no surprise that children with explosions can develop behavioral and emotional problems from being constantly frustrated. Even though there is no single known cause for explosions, many factors are confirmed to be involved.

CHAPTER 1
Explosive Child

Knowing the difference between a typical, antsy 4-year-old, and someone who is hyperactive to the extent that it affects his/her ability to learn is now tricky as attention deficit disorders are becoming more prevalent according to recent research.

A problem that manifests itself in persistent difficulty paying attention is recognized especially when a child is entering the world of school. Obviously, in this context, the difficulties related to the problem of concentration are often highlighted in an almost dramatic way. It is in the classroom that it becomes evident how keeping up with the demands of adults, internalizing general social and behavioral rules, carrying out assignments, respecting allotted time, simply listening to the teacher, and staying still in one's seat can become a problem. However, at this stage, it is absolutely important to look for clues that may allow you to recognize any difficulties your child or pupils may be having so that you can intervene at an early enough age. A young child may have behaviors that worry parents, but some of these (e.g., being peremptorily oppositional to requests, showing excessive and irrepressible vivacity, throwing too many tantrums) change and evolve with age, while others will remain unchanged or almost unchanged.

If we're having trouble coping with rage, knowing all of this can assist. We also need to be aware that parental rage might be harmful to young children because it motivates us to exercise self-control.

Some parents spanked their kids because of their upbringing. Simply because hitting has been practiced for generations does not make it right or a useful teaching technique. It causes physical, neurological, and mental wounds, and it must come to an end. We want to develop a loving link with our children, not break it, but the moment a parent raises his or her hand in anger, even if it's to "teach a lesson," we're destroying the exact bond we're trying to form. The most important lesson that children learn from physical punishment is that they can't trust or rely on their parents.

Those who were hit as children can still help to put a stop to this toxic legacy. Parents must first practice self-discipline before disciplining their children. Put some distance between what provokes you and how you respond so you don't lash out in anger or violence.

Some argue that hitting is acceptable if it leaves no trace, yet it leaves massive traces that last centuries. We can break the cycle.

If you're a parent, you're well aware that emotions can get the best of you at times. Children have an uncanny ability to push buttons you didn't even realize you had. Before you know it, you're screaming at the top of your lungs.

You're not alone in this, and your parental dissatisfaction is understandable. The good news is that you can adjust how you communicate with your children, moving away from a furious monologue and toward a respectful discourse.

The secret of good parents is that they know how to raise good children. Inside their thoughts, they have a whole other life. They uniquely communicate with their children. They uniquely converse with themselves. They're approaching the whole parenting process from a different angle.

The difficult aspect of parenting, as any parent knows, is regulating our anger triggers. Regardless of your child's specific issues, you must work on yourself if you want to be a good parent. The anger or anxiety that draws us into power battles is not caused by a child; it is caused by our fear and mistrust. Our early childhood traumas, whether large or tiny, are a part of who we are. They're also the part of us that takes control anytime we're disturbed, so you know that when you're angry or scared, it's usually always a horrible experience from your childhood that's driving your reactions.

We want our kids to be successful in life. Not in the sense of gaining the rewards that our society offers, but in the sense of discovering, polishing, and sharing their particular skills throughout their lifetimes. We also know how to assist children in doing so. Much of it has to do with how we manage our anger which allows our child to explore for himself and develop confidence and resilience.

Some children are born with temperaments that are more challenging to manage, and our inner work as parents is much more crucial for these children. But, no matter what your child brings, the way you respond to them when they come into the world will impact their ability to make the most of their life. Your child will amuse and frustrate you, thrill and annoy you in equal measure. Your child will ask you to grow as well, almost by mistake. You can raise happy, emotionally healthy children who are successful in every way if you can recognize when you're provoked and restore equilibrium before acting if you can ease your anxieties if you can reflect on your own experience and make peace with it.

CHAPTER 2

ASD Child's Explosions

A Checklist of ASD Red Flags

The Disorders within the Autism Spectrum

The disorders included in ASD are as follows:

Autistic Disorder

Children affected by an autistic disorder face issues forming normal relationships and communicating with others. Their range of interests and activities is limited. Symptoms vary greatly between patients. Strangely, the numbers of boys affected by an autistic disorder are five times that of girls.

Asperger Disorder

Called Asperger syndrome affects more boys than girls. Asperger patients have normal intelligence and their language capabilities develop early. However, their social skills are impaired, and cannot communicate effectively with others. Children with Asperger's disorder are known to have poor coordination, repetitive speech, difficulties with reading comprehension, math, written skills, obsession with some specified topic, and lack of common sense.

PDD-NOS

Pervasive Developmental Disorder-Not Otherwise Specified (or PDD-NOS) is called atypical autism. It is a neurological disorder that has some but not all attributes of Autistic Disorder. Children with PDD-NOS are known to have severe impairment in several spheres of development.

Childhood Disintegrative Disorder

This is a condition that occurs in 3–4-year-olds. The child's intellectual, social, and language skills are hit and deteriorate over several months. It is also called Heller's syndrome. Symptoms include loss of social skills, loss of bowel and bladder control, loss of motor skills, delay or lack of spoken language skills, inability to start and sustain oral communication, etc.

Rett's Disorder

This is seen in girls (mostly) between the ages of 6 and 18 months. It is characterized by wringing of the hands, slow head and brain growth, seizure, walking abnormalities, and mental retardation.

Children diagnosed with ASD face difficulties in the following areas:

- Communication and language
- Socialization
- Restricted interests, and
- Impairment in social collaboration
- Lack of fitting eye look
- Lack of warm, cheerful expressions
- Lack of offering interest or happiness
- Lack of reaction to the name
- Impairment in communication

- Lack of indicating signals
- Lack of coordination of nonverbal correspondence
- Unusual prosody
- Little variety in pitch
- Odd inflection
- Unpredictable mood
- Surprising voice quality
- Repetitive behaviors as well as restricted interests
- Repetitive developments with items
- Repetitive movements or posing of the body

Within the above areas, many different symptoms are manifested by ASD patients. Therefore two different ASD patients usually have a different set of behaviors and abilities.

The range of ASD symptoms is a broad one. Some speak in single words or short sentences, while some have great verbal skills. Some children are less sociable and like to be alone, while some like to socialize, but face challenges in socializing.

These children have a wide range of interests and repetitive behavior. Some children have an interest in unusual things like signboards, street signs, animals, plants, gardens, etc., while some have made it a hobby of collecting unusual objects like pencil sharpeners, erasers, etc.

In some cases, the interests of these children may not

be appropriate for their age and in terms of the intensity as well. For instance, a child has a knack for detailed information on a particular topic, and sometimes, they are known to have an extreme interest in only one item (like an unhealthy interest in one particular toy above all others).

Another common observation is that they have repetitive behaviors/mannerisms. They may be simple behaviors like the flapping of their hands or a more complex mannerism. The list may be endless.

It important thing is to remember and keep in mind that each child with ASD is unique and no two children would behave like each other. So, there is a need for personalized care for each ASD patient.

Roughly 1 out of every 85 children is born with ASD and boys are 5 times more likely to be affected than girls, going by the numbers.

If you think your kid may have Autism Spectrum Disorder, please read through the rundown of conceivable indications of ASD.

Your kid does not have to exhibit the greater part of the shown practices to allude to for an appraisal. Kindly note that these qualities might likewise be markers of different conditions. Conceivable early indications of ASD.

If your kid demonstrates two or a greater amount of these signs, please approach your pediatric human services supplier for a referral for an assessment. A screening apparatus called the M-CHAT (Modified Checklist for Autism in Toddlers) can likewise help you figure out whether an expert ought to assess your youngster. This straightforward autism screen takes just a couple of minutes. If the answers recommend your tyke is in danger of a mental imbalance, please counsel with your kid's specialist. In like manner, if you have some other worries about your youngster's advancement, don't hold up. Address your specialist now about screening your kids.

Individuals with a type of autism, called mentally unbalanced savantism, have outstanding aptitudes in particular territories, for example, music, craftsmanship, and numbers. Individuals with this type of mental imbalance perform these abilities without practice or lessons.

Due to the nature of the symptoms, Autism Spectrum Disorder is sometimes challenging to diagnose at an early age. If the child is the first, the parents have no experience to deal with. Seeing other toddlers and babies develop differently, they may start to worry. When expressing these concerns to relatives, friends, or neighbors, the parent will often hear things like, "It will grow out of it." Parents will sometimes talk to their doctor about their concerns about the child's lack of verbal communication and eye contact, his inability to respond to his name, and his obsessive attachment to specific objects.

In many cases, a baby will develop naturally and then begin to regress at around eighteen months. These children are generally easier to diagnose due to the apparent difference in past and present behaviors that parents and professionals can attest to by looking at photos, watching videos, and comparing observations. Some children have chronic ear infections; others may show allergic reactions. Many have intestinal problems: chronic diarrhea or chronic constipation. Or a child may have constant anger and/or sleepless nights. Parents can often be concerned because their child is a walking encyclopedia on a particular topic (such as trains), obsessively playing the same toy the same way, or only eating certain foods. Maybe it's the kindergarten teacher who notices that he or she doesn't seem to be engaging in conversation with her classmates and struggles with any changes in routine. Or a child may be considered "bad" at school because of certain behaviors, and perhaps the parents have not noticed anything wrong because he is an only child, or think that boys mature less quickly than girls. It may be accurate, but it's best to be safe and investigate your concerns.

The physician may hesitate to jump to any conclusions because not all reported observations are necessarily objective and may be interpreted differently. Everyone knows someone who talked late. On the other hand, a parent may not listen to concerns expressed by a childcare worker, teacher, or neighbor. It is unfortunate because the earlier the diagnosis, the sooner the surgery, the better the prognosis. Some people with Autism Spectrum Disorder can reach adulthood without ever being diagnosed. They may have always felt like they weren't on the same wavelength as others from a social, emotional, or sensory standpoint.

Behavioral Characteristics of the Autism Spectrum Disorder

- As a child, he or she does not reach out to be held by their mother or seek cuddles
- They do not imitate others
- Use the adult as a means to obtain the desired object, without interacting with the adult as a person
- Does not develop age-appropriate peer relationships
- Lack of spontaneous sharing of interests with others
- Difficulty mixing with others
- They prefer to be alone
- They have detached ways
- Little or no eye contact
- Detached from the feelings of others
- It does not develop speech or develop an alternative method of communication such as pointing and gesturing
- They have the word, and then lose it

- Repeat words or phrases instead of using everyday language
- Speak on very narrow topics
- Difficulty speaking abstract concepts lack or impairment of conversation skills
- Inappropriate attachment to objects
- Strange obsessive play with toys or objects (continuously aligns or turns)
- Dislikes change in routine or environment (furniture moved around the house)
- They will only eat certain foods
- Will only use the same item (same plate or cup, same clothes)
- Repetitive motor movements (rocking, hand flapping)
- Distinctive vocal characteristics (flat monotone or high pitch)
- It does not reach developmental milestones in a time frame or neurotypical sequence
- Low muscle tone
- Irregular fine and gross motor skills
- They cover the ears
- He or she doesn't respond to noise or name; they act deaf
- It does not react to pain
- It becomes stiff when held, dislikes being touched
- Become hyperactive or unresponsive in noisy or very bright environments
- Eat or chew unusual things
- Puts objects up to smell them
- Often removes clothes

- Hitting or biting themselves (hitting the head or slapping the thighs or chest)
- It spins like a top
- They have tantrums for no apparent reason, and it is difficult to calm down
- Hit or bite others
- Common sense is missing
- Doesn't seem to understand simple requests. Frequent diarrhea, upset stomach, or constipation

Many of these behaviors are the children's responses to how they are processing their surroundings.

Different analysts are exploring the likelihood that under specific conditions, a bunch of precarious qualities may meddle with mental health, bringing about a mental imbalance. Still, different analysts are researching issues amid pregnancy or conveyance and in addition ecological elements, for example, viral contamination, metabolic lopsided characteristics, and presentation to chemicals.

- **Genetic vulnerability:** A mental imbalance tends to happen more habitually than anticipated among children who have specific medical conditions, including delicate X disorder, tuberous sclerosis, innate rubella disorder, and untreated phenylketonuria (PKU). Some unsafe substances ingested amid pregnancy additionally have been connected with an expanded danger of Autism.
- **Ecological factors:** Examination shows different

variables other than the hereditary segment are adding to the ascent in expanding event of autism—for instance, ecological poisons like overwhelming metals, for example, mercury, which are more predominant than previously. Those with autism (or those in danger) may be vulnerable against such poisons, as their capacity to metabolize and detoxify these exposures may be compromised.

Parent Involvement

A collaborative partnership between home and school can be a blessing. Frequent opportunities for discussions and feedback about the child's individual learning needs can indeed make a big positive difference to your child's life. Make sure you are in regular touch with the school.

Explosive students have trouble transferring or generalizing knowledge and skills from one situation to another. Of course, the child gains most because of a collaborative home and school. For him, it means that the same skills and concepts are reinforced throughout (at home and school) and leaves little scope for any confusion. A lack of this kind of coordination might bring a lot of confusion to the child's life, often having to learn a separate set of instructions at home and school.

These are the main types of valuable information that parents and teachers can share:

- The developmental history of the child.
- Any important health issues.
- Information about the range of professionals and caregivers that have been involved in caring for the child.
- Likes, dislikes, sensory sensitivities, and special interests of the child.
- Knowledge about effective positive reinforces and motivators that work with the child.
- How the child has learned a particular skill at home.
- Behaviors and strategies that have been successful at home or in other environments.
- Performances as students over brief and long periods and different settings.
- Perspectives on the student's perspectives, and other useful information.

It is important to consider the format, information that needs to be shared, and other information that may be needed from parents on a day-to-day basis at the school. There should be strict guidelines for reporting any significant behavioral changes or events that need mention between home and school. Generally, the classroom teacher is responsible for the content of home-school communication. You may consider it a daily diary for the student. Things that should be included in the diary are like:

- Activities in which the student participated.
- Any new skill that was demonstrated to the child.

- The nature of play with classmates.
- Songs and stories of the day.
- New areas of learning.
- Upcoming events, trips, or any special interactions/participations.

Having a child with Autism Spectrum Disorder has a major impact on the family. In addition to the stress associated with bringing up a child who needs more attention and care, children with autism are not as friendly as other children and do not approach their parents in the same way as other children. This lack of spontaneous signs of affection on one's child is very difficult for a parent. Families often tend to isolate themselves due to concern about their child's socially inappropriate behavior or fear of being embarrassed by certain behaviors of the child or the extreme fatigue that most parents of children with Autism Spectrum Disorder suffer. Families stop doing what they did before. Single-parent families find themselves alone with their hands full and with no free time to continue living any kind of social life, increasing their isolation. Being a single parent, adoptive parent, stepparent, custodial parent, or grandparent raising a child with Autism Spectrum Disorder adds even more difficulty to an already precarious situation.

A marriage or relationship with a significant person can deteriorate due to additional stress, fatigue, and differences of opinion about how to handle certain situations. Often one or both parents have a hard time coming to terms with having this child and are in different parts of the pain cycle. Add to that seeking support and trying to get proper education for the child, and it's easy to see how many couples end up getting it over with. Siblings may suffer from being raised in a family with a child who has Autism Spectrum Disorder. Not only do they have a brother who is difficult to understand, has limited interests, and is not social; they also have to do with some pretty wild behavior. They also feel the stress their parents are under and the fact that inevitably more of the parents' attention is occupied by the sibling with Autism Spectrum Disorder. However, research indicates that there are also positive aspects of having a sibling on the spectrum.

Extended family members, such as grandparents, also have difficulty dealing with Autism Spectrum Disorder. Some refuse to face the facts; others don't know what to say or what to do. Again, as a parent, it is up to you to decide when and what information to share.

Guideline for Parents: Things You Have to Do to Support Your Child

Learn More about Autism Disorder

The more you think about a mental imbalance range issue, the better prepared you'll be to settle on educated choices for your tyke. Teach yourself about the treatment choices, make inquiries, and take part in all treatment choices.

Accept Your Child

As opposed to concentrating on how your mentally unbalanced kid is unique about other kids and what he or she is "missing," practice acknowledgment. Appreciate your child's exceptional idiosyncrasies, praise little triumphs, and quite contrast your kid with others. Feeling unequivocally cherished and acknowledged will help your tyke more than anything else.

Try Not to Give Up

It is difficult to foresee the course of a mental imbalance range issue. Try not to make a hasty judgment about what life will be similar to for your kid. Like others, individuals with a mental imbalance have a whole lifetime to develop and build up their capacities.

CHAPTER 3

ADHD Symptoms and the Nature of the Disorder

What Is ADHD?

Attention-Deficit Hyperactivity Disorder (ADHD) is one of the most common mental disorders affecting children. ADHD additionally impacts lots of adults. Signs of ADHD consist of inattentiveness (not having the ability to keep focused), hyperactivity (unusually or abnormally active), and impulsivity (rash acts that occur without thought).

An approximated 8.4% of children and also 2.5% of adults have ADHD. ADHD is usually diagnosed in school-aged children when it brings about disruption in the class or troubles with schoolwork; it is more common among boys than girls, and it can, likewise, impact adults.

Living with ADHD can be tough both for the parents and for the children. The good news is that it's possible to live very happily even with ADHD. As you will see in this book, there are plenty of things you can do as a parent to help your child grow healthier, stay more focused, and, generally, be better, both during childhood and as future adults.

Let's tackle what it doesn't mean. ADHD is not just a medical name for a child with a bit more energy than usual. All children have plenty of energy and that's a sign they are healthy, both mentally and physically.

However, when the energy is misplaced, too much, and it prevents the child from learning, growing up, and living a life similar to that of other children their age, it can become a problem.

Children and even teens with ADHD often have problems controlling their impulses, and paying attention are being one of the most obvious signs.

Such habits influence their schooling as well as life at home and their interaction with people and siblings. When this problem persists into adulthood, the adult ADHD person will display other signs such as having trouble managing time, scheduling time, establishing what needs to be worked on first, what is their priorities and also holding down a job. Problems with relationships, possibilities of addiction, and having low self-esteem could plague adults with ADHD.

Causes

Overall, it is unclear what truly causes ADHD. Each case is unique and can differ from the next. What your child is experiencing might be completely different than what another child is going through. According to research, genetics plays the biggest role in the cause of ADHD. It is much more common for a child to develop the disorder when it runs in the family. Since it is hereditary, this is not something that should be considered "contagious" or transmissible. For example, if your child is playing with other children in school, there is no risk of them passing ADHD on to those children.

To this day, scientists are still currently investigating how ADHD develops and what causes the disorder. There is plenty more research to be done. They have come to the conclusion that the genes present that typically lead to the development of ADHD include ones that are linked to the neurotransmitter dopamine—this is known as the neurotransmitter responsible for your memory, attention, and regulating body movements. Other research suggests exposure to certain chemicals as a child can contribute to the risk factor of developing ADHD. This theory is not 100% solidified, but it is thought to be a possible link to the disorder.

Those who do not monitor their children's sugar intake or technology time still need to be much more cautious. Above all, ADHD is a brain-based biological disorder. There is nothing that you can do to 100% prevent this from happening to any child, even your own. The good thing is that many children who do end up developing ADHD can still be very high-functioning individuals.

Symptoms of ADHD

The symptoms of ADHD, also known as attention deficit hyperactivity disorder, vary from child to child but usually include a mix of hyperactivity, inattention, and impulsivity.

Inattention

It is not that kids with ADHD cannot pay attention: they have no problem concentrating and staying on task while they are doing things they like or listening about topics they are interested in. They rapidly tune out when the job is monotonous or uninteresting.

Another typical issue is staying on track. Children with ADHD frequently go from task to task while not finishing any of them, or they skip stages in required processes. They have a tougher problem organizing their homework and time than typical children. When a lot is going on around them, kids with ADHD have difficulty concentrating; they typically require a calm, quiet atmosphere to stay focused.

The following are the most common indicators of inattention:

- Being easily distracted and having a limited attention span
- Making thoughtless errors—such as in homework
- Looking to be careless or misplacing items
- Being unable to concentrate on arduous or time-consuming activities
- Displaying an inability to listen to or follow directions
- Activity or endeavor that is continuously changing
- Having trouble managing daily chores
- Frequently avoids, resists, or is hesitant to

undertake things that demand sustained mental effort

- Frequently misplaces items required for jobs and activities (e.g., school materials, books, pencils, eyeglasses, tools).
- Is prone to becoming distracted

Hyperactive

Hyperactivity is the most evident symptom of ADHD. While many kids are naturally energetic, others who suffer from (ADHD) hyperactive attention deficit disorder are constantly going. They may attempt to accomplish many tasks at once, jumping from one activity to the next. Even when made to sit motionless, which might be difficult for them, they tap their foot, shake their leg, or drum their fingers.

Hyperactive children appear to be constantly moving. They cannot even sit still and will often run about or chat nonstop. Children with ADHD find it difficult to sit still and concentrate in class. They are free to move about the room, wriggle in their chairs, twitch their toes, touch anything, or tap a pencil loudly. Children with ADHD may experience extreme restlessness.

The following are the most common indicators of hyperactive:

- Frequently fidgets or taps their feet and hands or squirms in their seat. In circumstances where being seated is anticipated, the child often departs the seat.

- Kids find it difficult to sit still, play quietly, or relax. Move about a lot, probably running or climbing improperly.
- Excessive talking have a short fuse or a quick temper
- Frequently unable to play or participate in leisure activities in silence
- Frequently answers before the question have been fully answered

Diagnosis of the Symptoms

No ADHD test only can diagnose symptoms of attention deficit hyperactivity disorder. ADHD is a condition with three unique sub-types, signs that arrive along a spectrum of intensity, and overlapping comorbid conditions that often complicate analysis and treatment.

It takes a lot of test-taking, and evaluation to diagnose someone with ADHD. An assessment for ADHD can start with a visit to the doctor, but it won't end there. Generally, most doctors are not trained to diagnose ADHD and its symptoms. Only a few are trained to carry out the in-depth evaluation needed.

Worthwhile ADHD diagnosis would depend on the criteria described in the DSM-V. Diagnosis is conducted to check the patient's medical record, which is often accompanied by neuropsychological screening, it gives insight into the advantages and weaknesses, and helps identify comorbid and other conditions.

Many doctors explain that some patients' ADHD symptoms aren't noticed until later in life - this is true for people who have the inattentive type of ADHD.

Diagnosing a grown-up is trickier than diagnosing a youngster. The DSM-V sign guide is not useful in adults; almost all its steps are meant for diagnosing children. An ADHD medical diagnosis in adults takes place in a careful and scientific observation conducted by an ADHD specialist who takes his/her time during the evaluation.

"The DSM-V requirements are centered on research for children aged four to seventeen," says DARKISH, assistant clinical professor of psychiatry at Yale College and University School of Medication. As a result of this, most clinicians relax the standards when it comes to age. Recent research implies that in some people, symptoms are not obvious until adolescence when self-management problems surface in. Doctors may also diagnose adults who have just 4 or 5 symptoms if the symptoms are critical.

Associated Conditions of ADHD

As if a diagnosis of ADHD is not enough for a parent to worry about, there are often other conditions that develop in conjunction with ADHD or only as a reaction to ADHD. Children with ADHD and an associated disorder require much more time, attention, and medical care. It is believed that about half of all people with ADHD also have another need. The Centers for Disease Control and Prevention estimates that about 2/3 of ADHD children have another disorder in children. Associated conditions can be mild or severe. They might be directly linked to ADHD, or they might be in a condition that has simply taken its time to show up and announce its presence. These additional conditions fall within two categories: secondary conditions and comorbid conditions.

Secondary conditions are those that are a direct result of ADHD. When a child is dealing with ADHD, it is quite frustrating and stressful. In many cases, other conditions develop because they are triggered by frustration and stress. As treatment of ADHD progresses, these secondary conditions often become more manageable or fade away entirely. Comorbid conditions are conditions that exist concurrently with ADHD. They are not going out with ADHD treatment. Comorbid conditions usually need a specific treatment program. You and your child's doctor must determine which additional conditions are secondary or comorbid.

The number of associated conditions a child or adult can have along with ADHD is endless. There simply is not enough time or book space to discuss every possible medical condition because they are not all definitively associated with ADHD. However, it is essential to know some common disorders and their possible symptoms because knowledge is power for ADHD. While not an all-inclusive list of probably related conditions, the following list describes many more prevalent associated conditions:

Anxiety

We have all felt a little anxious at some point in our lives. Anxiety manifests itself as feelings of stress, worry, tension, tiredness, and several other symptoms. However, the fleeting pressure the average person feels is not considered a disorder. Chronic anxiety affects about 30% of ADHD children and approximately 50% of ADHD adults. These feelings of worry and stress can have a detrimental effect on the nature of life. Whether or not the anxiety begins to diminish with ADHD treatment determines if it is a secondary or comorbid condition.

Depression

Everyone feels sad from time to time. Depression is a severe disorder that involves handling unhappiness, moodiness, irritability, and even worthlessness. These feelings do not go away. Depression affects more than just your mood—it reduces your interest in life. It requires treatment, often including therapy. Depression may occur because of ADHD or because of environmental factors and genetic predisposition. In most cases, it is considered a comorbid condition.

When children have difficulty functioning, particularly when they have challenges at school due to ADHD, they may feel depressed and hopeless. As a result, people with ADHD have trouble paying attention and organizing them, exacerbated when sadness is present.

Comorbid depression affects around 10-15 percent of children with ADHD. Due to a loss of self-worth, these patients frequently develop suicidal thoughts.

Learning and Language Disabilities

As many as 50% of ADHD children have a type of learning disorder. When compared to only 5% of non-ADHD children having learning disorders, this number is quite compelling. Dyslexia and dyscalculia are two of the most common learning syndromes that may affect an ADHD child. Dyslexia has an impact on the child's ability to read and write. Dyscalculia impacts the child's ability to understand and perform math skills. Language disorders affect approximately 12% of ADHD children, while these speech problems only affect about 3% of non-ADHD children. Both learning and language disabilities fall into the category of comorbid conditions. They each require their treatment plan.

Gross and Fine Motor Skill Difficulties

Fine motor skills include tasks like grasping a pencil with your fingers and writing. Gross motor skills include physical activities, such as jumping and running. Both types of gifts require the use of certain small or large sets of muscles. ADHD can affect the fine and gross motor skills of your child. For example, you may notice that your child struggles to write neatly because his/her hand and fingers jerk around. Your child may seem awkward and overly clumsy, such as falling frequently or struggling to do a jumping jack, because ADHD affects larger sets of muscles. These disorders are comorbid conditions and require their treatment plan.

Obsessive-Compulsive Disorder

The obsessive-compulsive disorder, also known as OCD, may have you thinking of the hoarding shows on television. While hoarding certainly is a symptom of OCD, it is not the only symptom. This disorder can be mild or extreme. It can manifest itself in repetitive behavior, like counting to a certain number while performing a task or even pulling out hair. OCD can also involve the extreme need to be clean, such as washing hands repeatedly, even until they are raw. OCD may involve hoarding, which is the overwhelming desire to collect certain items, or it is a form of extreme anxiety to the point of being overly cautious. OCD is also a comorbid condition. Treatment can be helpful, along with possible medications.

Oppositional Defiant Disorder

The oppositional defiant disorder is a common condition associated with ADHD and known as ODD. This disorder results in extreme bouts of anger and rage. That is not a typical temper tantrum. ODD is an uncontrollable anger/outrage that occurs during a meltdown that results from even the smallest trigger. These meltdowns can last just a few minutes or even as long as half an hour. When an ODD child has a breakdown, he or she is usually quite remorseful about what happened once he or she has calmed down. This disorder can be secondary or comorbid. There are various types of treatment available.

Bipolar Disorder

Bipolar disorder is another mood disorder that has various symptoms. It is a comorbid disorder, so you cannot expect ADHD treatment to fix the bipolar problem. Bipolar disorder often includes severe and unexplainable mood swings. For example, your child may be ecstatic and extremely happy for several days, only to suddenly switch gears to anger and rage that also lasts for several days. People with bipolar disorder have a hard time relaxing and calming down, especially when they are in a "manic" state of mind. There are numerous medical treatments to help control bipolar disorder because even though the "highs" feel significant to the patient, the "lows" may feel worse than anything they have ever felt—possibly driving them to the point of suicide.

Tic Disorder

A tic disorder involves the physical twitching of certain groups of muscles. These muscles are often found in the face, neck, and shoulder areas of the body. You may notice short, jerking movements of your child's head that he or she cannot stop or control. You may detect tics in the eyes or mouth, such as rapid and uncontrolled eye blinking or a chronic twitch at the corner of the mouth. Tics are most often noticed in children, and many children ultimately grow out of the tic disorder as they become an adult. It was once believed that certain stimulant ADHD medications caused tic disorders. However, more has been learned about these types of conditions, including the fact that there is a genetic factor to consider. It is now believed that the stimulant medications did not cause the tic disorder. The drug flipped on the internal, genetic predisposition switch residing within the child. Tic disorders are comorbid disorders and can be managed with appropriate treatment.

Tourette Syndrome

That is a syndrome that most people misunderstand. A person hears the word Tourette, and they automatically assume that the afflicted will randomly yell out swear words. That is not a movie—this is real life. It is interesting to note that about 60–80% of people with this particular syndrome also have ADHD, but not even 10% of ADHD people have Tourette syndrome. Tourette syndrome does vocally manifest itself. Think of it like tics, and only it is tics of the vocal cords. People with this disorder may make odd noises randomly or repeat phrases indiscriminately, including the occasional swear word. However, uncontrolled swearing is not a realistic description of Tourette syndrome. That is a comorbid condition that requires a different treatment plan than ADHD.

Abuse of Substances

Studies have indicated that ADHD children have a higher risk of smoking cigarettes at an early age. They also have an added chance of following this nicotine dependence with alcohol abuse and, in severe cases, even drug abuse. ADHD children are twice as likely to develop an addiction to nicotine. It is necessary to note that studies show ADHD children treated with stimulant medications are less likely than their non-ADHD peers to abuse illegal stimulants, such as cocaine and methamphetamine. That may be a result of the opposite effect that stimulants have on ADHD children. These substance abuse problems are a secondary result of ADHD. In many cases, with the appropriate treatment, parents can be proactive and prevent substance abuse from ever becoming a problem by actively treating ADHD.

Conduct Disorder

Conduct disorder is a pattern of conduct in children who repeatedly violate others' rights or basic social standards. The child often displays these behavior patterns in several contexts, including at home, school, and in social interactions, and they cause considerable impairment in social, academic, and familial functioning. A high level of uncontrollable aggressiveness characterizes this condition. Children with CD are more prone to injure themselves and others severely. They have a propensity for breaking regulations and causing intentional harm to others' belongings.

Around 25% of children with ADHD have been identified with at least one behavioral or conduct disorder. Early treatment, as usual, may make a huge difference.

Mood Disorders

ADHD individuals have a co-occurring mood disorder in about 38% of cases. Extreme mood swings are a symptom of mood disorders. Children who suffer from mood disorders may appear to be in a poor mood all of the time. For no apparent reason, they may weep every day or be angry with others regularly. Depression, bipolar illness, and seasonal allergies have been more frequent in persons with ADHD of all ages. Around 14 percent of children with ADHD are thought to have co-occurring mental problems. It is critical to keep an eye out for indications of these diseases and get treatment if necessary.

Autism Spectrum Disorders

Autism Spectrum Disorders encompass a wide spectrum of conditions marked by difficulty with communication, social skills, routine changes, repetitive behaviors, and how children perceive different senses. Many of the symptoms that are found in ADHD are also observed in ASD. It is believed that around a third of kids diagnosed with ADHD also fulfill ASD criteria. Furthermore, having an ADHD diagnosis has been proven to postpone the diagnosis of Autism by up to three years.

Treatment of Conditions Linked with ADHD

When a child has both ADHD and a co-occurring disorder, a health care provider may choose to treat the ADHD first since primary treatment of ADHD can reduce stress, increase attentional resources, and improve the child's capacity to manage the signs of the other condition. Medication, behavior therapy, skill training, counseling, and educational supports and adjustments are all possibilities for ADHD treatment. These treatments can be customized to the children and family-specific requirements. They can assist the patient in controlling symptoms, coping with the condition, improving general psychological well-being, and managing social interactions.

CHAPTER 4

7 Strategies to Positive Parenting and Managing an Explosive Child

Help Your Child but Set Limits

We always want to rescue our children whenever they're in a rush. It can harm their independence. The more you do things for your children, the more they will rely on you and the less they'll do for themselves.

Be supportive, but let your child do specific tasks by himself. For instance, when it comes to homework, encourage him to work on it without your help. If you have to monitor him, then don't hover. Sit near him, and work on your own. It is an excellent time to tackle unfinished reports, update your blog, and the like.

Practice Patience

Patience is a quality that all parents require, but it is significant for parents of children with explosions. While it is natural for parents to "solve" their children's problems and "cure" their explosions, most children require time to develop. According to NIMH and other studies, children with explosions develop similarly to their peers, except for brain development, where they lag by about three years. According to these studies, parents can be confident that their children will eventually develop the necessary organizational, planning, and judgment skills demonstrated by children who do not have behavioral disorders. However, the slower maturation path may necessitate more patience and a focus on long-term development rather than quick fixes.

Get Down to Their Level

What this means is that you need to take a look at the situation from your child's perspective. Just because you see things one way does not mean that your child sees them the same way. For starters, you are a lot older with much more life experience. This combined with the explosive disorders factor can make things very hard to identify with if you simply compare their experience to your own. Quit the comparisons, and do your best to understand where your child is coming from. This is going to make your child feel seen and respected for who they are.

Create a Healthy Environment

The environment that you create in your home affects your child tremendously. You already know this, but it will become even more evident as your child grows up. Make sure the entire household is a healthy and stable place that your child knows they are safe in. If there is any uncertainty or toxicity, you should know that this is going to affect your child. Directly or subconsciously, these instances will affect their behavior and possibly trigger their disorder explosions symptoms. You can create a healthier home environment by controlling who gets to visit the home. If you know that certain people are not the best influences on your child, then you should not let them into your environment. It sounds harsh, but it is a simple solution that will save your child a lot of hassle as they grow up. You cannot punish your child for acting out if this is the behavior that they are seeing from other people in your household.

If you find that someone who is already living under your roof is causing issues, you need to set that person aside and have a talk with them about how their behavior disrupts the environment. Make sure they do not feel attacked by explaining how everyone who is living under the same roof will benefit from behaving better. This is the best thing you can do to ensure that you are keeping an overall stable and loving household environment.

Keep Things Positive

Even when you are shelling out the discipline, you do not need to approach things negatively. Your child already knows that they did something wrong and that they are being taught a lesson. You can do so in a no confrontational way. By approaching the lesson in this way, your child is going to see that they can treat others the same. Make sure that you remain aware of your tone when you are teaching your child something that you want them to do or correcting their behavior—a lighthearted but firm tone makes a difference. Your instructions are already clear, so there is no reason to harp on your child for why they are not following them or why they messed up. You know that their explosive disorders can be very challenging to deal with. Instead, you should focus on the solution.

Communicate with Teachers and Other Professionals

Communicate openly and honestly with your child's teachers and other adults who interact with your child, such as camp counselors. Children with explosive disorders have a legal right to special school accommodations, such as an Individualized Education Program (IEP), to help them succeed. Many parents, however, try to conceal the diagnosis of a behavioral disorder for fear of stigmatizing their child. Teachers and others in teaching and caregiving roles may assume a child is willfully defiant or disruptive if they are unaware of the diagnosis. If you communicate openly about your child's difficulties, teachers will be able to work with him or her more effectively. Parents should not request that their children be excused from assignments. Instead, they should consult with teachers about how to assist their children in completing their schoolwork.

Research More about Explosive Disorders

Parents need to understand their children's behavior to help them fight the battle. That's why there is a variety of support groups for parents who have children with explosive disorders. Aside from that, there's an influx of reliable sources on the Internet to help you figure out your child.

When you know more, you'll find out that you're able to handle the situation better. You can anticipate problems that might lead to potentially harmful behavior.

CHAPTER 5

SLEEPING TIME

Sleep is one of those things that we all need. However, with explosives kids, sleep is invaluable. If they don't get enough, they will become emotionally unstable. Their working memories will deteriorate, their behaviors will worsen, their information processing will go into disarray—everything is affected by sleep. To facilitate sleep, make sure the child gets some exercise during the day or morning. Make sure to keep the kid from engaging in video games or T.V. watching at least 20–30 minutes before bedtime. Choose earplugs, use a clock that doesn't have bright lights on it, and make sure to turn the child's bed away from the door so that light seeping through doesn't keep him or her awake. Parents can also put opaque curtains to blanket light from outside. Read a bedtime story, give the child a favorite animal or blanket, make sure the room temperature is cooler rather than warmer, make sure scratchy tags on pajamas are removed, make sure they cover their feet if they are cold, and ensure your child envisions calming images like counting sheep or floating feathers. All of these strategies will help the child ease to sleep.

Difficulty sleeping is very common with explosive disorders. It isn't clear whether it is related to explosions themselves or if it is co-occurring. Another common effect of explosive disorders medicines used with young children is poor sleep. Because many disorder medications are stimulants chemically related to amphetamine, they can have a disruptive effect on sleep. It is recommended that parents discuss this and other negative potential side effects of medications before starting your young child on medications.

Helping Your Toddler Sleep

There are some very effective ways to help your toddler sleep. One simple step is to make sure your child gets exercise every day. If they can go outside, running, skipping, riding bikes are all great ways to blow off some steam. Indoor physical activities include dancing, calisthenics, or yoga.

It is also essential that toddlers eat healthy meals. Foods high in fiber and protein are the most desirable. Fresh vegetables, fruit along with beans, fish, and meat should be provided regularly. Avoid sweetened breakfast cereals and sugary drinks. Naturally sweet mint and chamomile tea are a good alternative. Caffeinated beverages have been used for decades to reduce the extreme hyperactivity and impulsivity associated with explosive disorders.

Establish a routine schedule for going to bed and napping. Create predictable and calming pre-bedtime routines. This can include reading, massage, quiet games, and listening to soft music. You can also dim the lights and create white noise. White noise is sound containing many different frequencies of equal intensity.

There are other excellent strategies for helping your toddler get the sleep they need. It's a good idea to turn off bright TV, computers and video games. These can easily become sources of distraction. Take these screened electronic devices out of your child's room. Most toddlers have figured out how to turn these devices on by themselves. For many explosive children, turning these devices on at odd hours of the night is just too tempting, and your child will pay the price in sleep deprivation, the effects of which can be hyperactivity and impulsivity.

Magic breathing and patience stretching are two more valuable techniques that can help your child sleep. Magic breathing is simply a deep breathing technique.

Getting adequate sleep is an enormous benefit to the body and brain. The evidence for this is very strong. Regulating mood and sustaining long periods of concentration are made possible by attaining restful, restorative sleep. There is also good evidence that adequate sleep will fuel learning. The brain is highly active at night, collecting and rerunning what is learned throughout the previous day.

Once bad sleeping habits are difficult to unlearn. Your child may have behavioral issues that appear every evening when it is time to go to bed. A preteen may be trying to cope with anxieties each night, or they may become defiant about getting ready for bed. Being the enforcer of a proper sleep schedule for your child may be exhausting.

A Plan for Proper Sleep

You can change your child's dysfunctional sleep and bedtime habits by implementing these three steps:

1. **Remove the screens.** This means taking all the electronic devices with screens out of the room designated for sleep. TVs, computers, phones, and video games should all be put in a separate room. If this is not feasible, then the screens should be covered during bedtime. An hour before bedtime begins, you can place the covers over each screen.
2. **Establish a bedtime routine.** It is recommended that it be predictable, lasting 30 to 60 minutes and at the same time every day. It never should be hurried or under pressure. This is a time to let your preteen child relax. The routine should always be predictable. For example, you might tell a bedtime story, or you and your child might softly sing a favorite song.
3. **Provide behavior therapy.** If your child has severe sleeping problems, they will benefit from behavior therapy specifically designed to improve their sleeping habits. The cost of these programs is typically lower than traditional behavioral therapy, and very often, parents see improvements in their child's sleeping habits in just a day.

The Importance of Exercise

Exercise has a more significant impact on behavioral disorders symptoms than food, according to studies. Yet, adjustments in diet and nutrition are more commonly promoted as a treatment for explosive disorders.

Activities outdoors can include running, bike riding, swimming, and competitive sports. You can serve as a coach and mentor. Find a local park with a basketball court or a baseball diamond. Perhaps you can teach your child the game and give them an outlet for releasing pent-up energy at the same time. Indoor activities can include dance, jumping rope, ping pong, and calisthenics. The main thing is to always structure each day to allow for physical activities. Your preteen may tell you which activities appeal to them the most, and it is good to allow them a choice.

A good night's sleep is essential for both physical and mental health. We spend roughly a third of our lives sleeping, but we might get tired and have trouble concentrating when we do not get enough sleep. Sleep issues are extremely frequent and one of the most common health concerns in children with explosive disorders is.

There are several methods for assisting short-tempered children in falling asleep more effortlessly. They are as follows:

Before Going to Bed, Respond to the Child's Requirements

Children will occasionally employ delaying techniques to avoid going to bed. For example, you may ask to use the restroom or for food or water. Taking care of these requirements before bedtime as part of a routine will help you recognize and avoid these delay tactics.

Try these things before putting a child to bed:

- Ensuring that they have eaten enough food— Caffeine-containing items, such as chocolate and cola, should be avoided.
- Bringing a cup of water to their bedside
- Sending them to the restroom
- Assisting the kid in learning to use the restroom independently at night

Lowering Anxiety and Caregiver Reliance

Some children perceive that falling asleep is dependent on parents or caretakers. They might want someone to soothe them to sleep or lay next to them as they sleep. They may also employ delaying tactics to keep their parents around for a longer period.

Children may act out because they are scared of unpleasant nightmares, the dark, or their caregiver abandoning them. Separation anxiety is the term for this. It is common in young children, and it can last until adulthood.

Reduced sleep anxiety might help children feel less reliant on adults. Try:

- Putting up a nightlight
- Providing a comfort object for the kid, such as a teddy animal
- Demonstrating relaxing methods to them
- Not in the evening, but throughout the day, chatting with them over their concerns
- Using the progressive extinction approach, gradually encourage a kid to become used to being apart from caretakers.
- Seek medical advice about cognitive behavioral therapy if your child has any nocturnal anxieties or phobias stopping them from sleeping.
- Creating a conducive sleeping environment

Create a sleep environment that is peaceful, cool, and quiet as much as possible. Allow the kid to assist you with this since they can tell parents what helps them feel safe and comfortable. This could imply:

- Rearranging objects so that they do not cast ominous shadows

- Relocating the bed to a different location in the room
- Allowing the youngster to select his or her bedding or pajamas
- Eliminating distracting items from their environments, such as ticking clocks or displays

Keeping a Regular Schedule

A regular bedtime routine might make it easier for youngsters to fall asleep. Try:

- Confirming that the child's bedtime is age-appropriate
- Even on weekends, keep to the same sleep pattern.
- Brushing one's teeth, combing one's hair, or listening to a bedtime table simultaneously every night
- In the hours coming up to sleep, avoid excessively stimulating activities, such as playing video games or watching TV.

Implementing a Sleep Hygiene Strategy

Instead of being a place for more play activities or punishment, make the child's sleeping space or bedroom a place for peaceful activities and rest time solely. This helps to maintain sleep hygiene and strengthens the link between sleep and the bedroom.

Similarly, try to keep kids from watching TV or completing homework in bed. If a kid is accustomed to using devices until night, gradually reduce their time spent on screens until they stop 5 minutes before bedtime, and then increase it to 10 minutes, and so on.

If a kid frequently wakes up throughout the night or early morning, rather than lying in bed unable to sleep, they should get up doing something uninteresting until they fell asleep again. If the kid wakes up, try pointing out some peaceful activities that they can do independently. Some possibilities include:

- A book is being read
- Listening to a recorded book
- Relaxing while listening to music
- Developing good midday habits

Changing your behavior during the day might also help you sleep better. Someone may try:

- Avoiding all caffeine sources, such as cola, chocolate, tea, and coffee
- Encouraging children to engage in physical activity early in the day
- Putting off calm, peaceful activities until later in the day or later in the evening.

CHAPTER 6

Looking at the Bright Side of Being a Parent of an Explosive Child

Accepting Your Child's Behavioral Disorders

Dealing with an explosive child can be highly stressful and frustrating so try to learn as much as possible about explosive disorders and do everything you can to help your child and yourself. It may be more difficult for you if you are the primary caregiver, but don't forget that stress can affect your entire family. You must devise strategies to assist you and your family in coping with and accepting the situation.

Creating Healthy Expectations

First of all, I want you to release the idea that there is not only one way to be happy and fulfilled. Secondly, let go of your current expectations and become more flexible in the image you have for your child. Instead of the life, you had initially pictured, visualize a realistic future for them that would enable your child to reach their fullest potential, one that you as a family collective can help to shape and influence to bring out their best. If your child can, involve them in this stimulating process so they can have a hands-on role in creating the dream for their future, too. Make it fun, make it interesting, and gather as much input from them as possible. If your child is not able, consider involving their doctors or therapists in your vision to get a more robust understanding of what a realistic and reasonable image looks like in the first place.

When you have genuine expectations for your child, you can break down the ultimate dream into smaller achievable goals for you and your child to work toward. This is the big difference between realistic and unrealistic expectations. If you were parenting with unrealistic expectations, for example, you could open up a life of ongoing frustration, stress, and sadness as your child cannot reasonably meet those expectations. When you parent with realistic expectations, however, you see lovely progress toward those goals, and you begin to feel a sense of pride, accomplishment, and fulfillment with your child. That positive energy will be felt by your child, too, and it will lead to greater harmony between the two of you, as well as a deeper bond that you can both share. This energy will further increase the level of success you experience with parenting your child and aiding them in becoming the best they can be.

How to Cope Emotionally as a Parent

Let's be honest. It is incredibly upsetting to learn that your child has an explosive disorder. You might have guessed it. You may have thought that the symptoms and behavior your child has been exhibiting are symptoms of some disorder. Nonetheless, the doctor's official diagnosis is always a surprise.

The following are the most effective methods for overcoming emotional conflict and finding peace in acceptance:

- **Allow yourself to be sad.** As parents, we all have lofty expectations for our children: they will be well-behaved, high achievers in school, popular with their peers, and praised by teachers. When a child has diagnosed with an explosive disorder, this vision is shattered. It breaks your heart to realize that he will never behave like other children. Allow yourself time to grieve and avoid burying your emotions. It's OK to cry and be sad. The only way to get rid of these feelings is to acknowledge them.

- **Stop rejecting your child for who they are.** Your initial thoughts will most likely be angry: "Why can't my child be like everyone else?" Recognize but don't believe those thoughts. Instead, confront the beliefs.

- **Consider the following.** Do you love your child any less because they have a behavioral disorder? Do you hold them responsible for it? You probably love them even more and want to do everything you can to protect and shelter them. You adore your child regardless of who they are. It is another step in the right direction.

- **Recognize your child's positive qualities and be thankful that they are healthy and robust.** The explosive disorder does not preclude a child from being gifted and talented in a variety of areas. Because of their natural vitality and energy, those children are highly gifted and creative. Concentrate on these assets and allow them to become a source of pride and joy for you.

- **Don't feel bad about yourself.** When parents learn that a child has a disease or disorder, their first reaction is usually guilt. Your initial reaction will be that you are somehow responsible, which is natural. The only advice I can give you here is brief and to the point. You are not to blame. Let it go!

- **Come to a halt whenever you find yourself fighting reality.** Refusing to accept the fact is a losing battle. When you find yourself against hope, your child will not suddenly change their behavior, nor will their symptoms disappear. You may even deny that they are sick at all, believing that it was a misdiagnosis, and rush to seek a second and third opinion.

- **Ignoring the facts is emotionally damaging because an explosive child will never outgrow it and never behave like you expect them to.** When you notice yourself having these thoughts, stop right away and bring yourself back to reality. Your child requires your assistance and support, not your wishful thinking.

The goal of this is to shift your perspective to the process and accept your child's condition emotionally. Only then will you be able to move forward and stand up for yourself and your family.

Now that you've reached a point of acceptance, it's time to implement more practical coping strategies.

Take control of your stress. As a parent, the most difficult challenge you will face for an explosive child is stress. It is something you will have to deal with daily. Unless you have stress-reduction techniques in place, the consequences for your physical and mental health can be severe.

Every day, set aside time for yourself to unwind and relax. Meditate, do yoga, exercise, and go for a quiet walk or soak in a warm bath. While your child is at school, engage in a hobby or go out for a quiet lunch with friends; whatever helps you relax should be done regularly to avoid burnout. It is not a luxury but rather necessary, especially if you juggle a demanding career with a challenging family life.

Stress management will also help you be more tolerant and calmer when dealing with your child and less prone to rage or frustration. The less drama you can avoid, the better it will be for both you and your child.

Participate in a support group. Encouragement and support from other parents in a similar situation are essential. Look for these groups online or on social media platforms—you'll be surprised at how many there are. It is a fantastic way to share your problems and concerns with other parents and exchange advice, tips, and experiences.

If the group is close by, you can even plan to meet

regularly and introduce your children to one another. Many support groups also host expert lectures to keep members up to date on the latest information on explosive disorders. They also organize family activities and outings.

Change Starts with You (The Parent)

Parenting your child correctly, regardless of whether your child is neurotypical or lives with a behavioral disorder, means you have to create a parenting style that matches the needs of your child. Many first-time parents believe that they can choose their parenting style in advance and that their technique will automatically suit their child simply because that is the parenting style that feels best for them.

Your child will come out with their personality, preferences, strengths, weaknesses, and needs. You, as the parent, must create an adaptable parenting style that meets those needs so you can empower your child to grow up to be the best version of themselves they can be. For parents of neurotypical children, the example of how they want their children to become seems pretty clear-cut. For parents of children with behavioral disorders, your expectations may be different based on the level of ability that your child has.

Tips for Helping Your Family Cope

If you have other children, the first thing you should do is inform them that one of their siblings has a kind of behavioral disorder. Depending on their ages, simplify as needed. Explain that you must all work together to assist their sibling, as he may not always behave in the same manner as they do.

Tell them that you expect them to assist their brother or sister whenever possible and to never, ever make fun of his or her condition. When this is done, never be afraid to impose strict discipline.

The entire family should implement the strategies listed below. Lead by example, and your other children will learn to behave and interact with their siblings in the same way.

Highlight the "benefits" of this disorder. Children with this disorder frequently have unique talents that can be nurtured and developed. Some examples include creativity, spontaneity, energy, and enthusiasm. Make a point of pointing out these gifts to your child regularly.

Assist your child whenever possible. For instance, when he is struggling with a particular task. Encourage your family to assist with homework and to attend therapy sessions whenever possible.

Establish family and household rules and activities that will help your child succeed. Giving them shorter chores to complete, for example, or making a list of things they need to do so that they can cross each one off as they meet them. Structure and schedule playtime with siblings so that they can participate in the games they enjoy.

If possible, keep an eye on playtimes to ensure that the child does not become overly excited. Keep an eye out for fights between siblings or other children and intervene immediately. When assigning larger tasks, enlist the assistance of a sibling to assist your child in completing them.

Accepting Mistakes as an Opportunity to Learn

You, like every other parent, are bound to make mistakes. You have probably already made thousands by now, and there will be plenty more as you continue your journey of parenting. Even parents of adult children make mistakes and find themselves having to recover from those mistakes in one way or another, as mistakes are a natural part of raising children. As they say, children do not come with a manual.

Rather than punishing yourself for making mistakes, or having an unrealistic outlook of your ability to parent without making mistakes, you need to accept the fact that mistakes are inevitable. You will make mistakes many times over, whether you like it or not. Sometimes, you will become overwhelmed and will have difficulty regulating your emotions. Other times, you might miss an important clue, and it could lead to your child having a meltdown and your environment lacking the peace you strive to create. There are many ways that mistakes can be made, and many reasons why those mistakes may be made. Regardless of how they happen, though, you must understand that they are inevitable.

Learn to adapt to each situation, developing new strategies for how you will minimize the impact of your errors on future experiences. Shift your perspective to view mistakes as an opportunity to learn and grow as a parent. Every time you overreact, miss a cue or have a negative experience with parenting, reflect on why that happened, and what contributed to your negative experience. See if you can identify the trigger, the moment where everything went wrong, and what could have been done to prevent that situation or reverse it once it started. When you use mistakes as motivation for learning, it becomes easier to forgive yourself and navigate any new challenges thrown at you in a more prepared, productive, and calm state if similar situations were to arise.

Take Care of Yourself

Ask for help from family members and close friends when you need some time off. You must have alone time to help you manage the stress.

Find ways to help reduce stress:

- Reading books
- Watching a movie
- Having a cup of coffee in a quiet place

Your health is important; getting enough rest, eating the right food, and exercising keep you healthy and strong.

Best of all, cut yourself some slack and understand that you are not a magician, nobody's perfect, and know the value of a reliable support system.

Putting Your Safety Mask on First

As the parent of a child with a behavioral disorder, you have likely been presented with many situations where you had to defend your child in unusual ways. You have had to protect your child mentally, emotionally, and physically from many involvements they have encountered that are not ordinary experiences for neurotypical children. Perhaps you have protected them by drastically adjusting their environment, dealing with bullies at daycare/school, or fending off fellow adults that do not comprehend your child or your parenting experience at all. All of these occurrences can be exhausting and seemingly never-ending when you are protecting your child. They can also leave you forgetting to tend to yourself and your own emotions as you become absorbed with protecting your child from the world around them.

Increasing Your Feelings of Gratitude

Upon confronting chronically challenging situations, it can be easy to develop negative mindsets toward those circumstances. With parenting your child, you may have negative emotions toward parenting, the day-to-day experiences you have with your child, or even your child themselves. Again, these are only feelings caused by troubling emotions, and they do not reflect the way you truly feel about your child. Still, if they linger long enough, it can make the entire experience of parenting far more frustrating and can damage your relationship with your child, as well as the way you behave toward and around your child.

Taking time to regularly express appreciation for your child's existence and for the opportunity as a parent is an important way to counter those negative feelings so that you can create a more realistic and positive parenting experience. Each day, express gratitude to yourself and your child.

CHAPTER 7
Behavioral Therapy for Explosive Children

Often abbreviated to CBT, this kind of treatment is perfect for parents wishing to be closely involved and active in their child's clinical development. CBT's focus is to train parents and other caregivers in the management of children's explosive symptoms.

One of the characteristics of being the parent of an explosive child is that it raises many doubts, irrational thoughts, and expectations. While other therapies focus on direct actions, CBT helps you eliminate the roadblocks that prevent you from helping your child overcome his symptoms of explosivity.

Cognitive-behavioral therapy is one of the most effective types of psychotherapy. It aims to help a child change his or her behavior by managing daily reactions and actions. It usually involves practical assistance that seeks to establish tasks, complete schoolwork, and manage emotionally difficult situations. Behavioral therapy also instructs children to self-regulate. That enables a child to give him or herself praise or rewards for acting accordingly. By doing this, a child can think before acting and avoid rash actions. That includes parents and teachers who can give the child positive or negative feedback for certain actions. Delineated and structured chores, lists, and rules may facilitate this process.

Well-implemented cognitive behavioral therapy will not only strive to change behaviors. It will seek to transform the very thinking processes that birth these behaviors. In short, cognitive-behavioral therapy is a unique approach to treating an explosive disorder naturally and sustainably. It allows children to evaluate how they feel. Why do they act the way they do? Why does one stimulus make them feel bad when another does not? How do classmates and teachers affect their moods? What do they think to themselves when negative feelings arise? How about when positive feelings occur? Ultimately, what can they do to ensure that when things go badly, they don't go that badly?

Therapists can also teach children social skills, including how to wait their turn, request help, share personal property, and respond appropriately to criticism. Children can even learn how to read body language, such as facial expressions and voice tone. That will enable them to understand more clearly social nuances and to act more appropriately for their age.

This therapy focuses on how behavior is affected by thoughts. Parents and therapists agree on the number of sessions a child needs before they are ready to adapt their behavior without constant sessions.

What does this form of therapy help the child with?

- It controls impulsivity and helps children develop self-control
- Works on defiance and aggression and provides a coping mechanism and effective problem-solving skills.

- Helps with self-esteem issues and thus improves self-image issues.

The Cognitive Behavior Therapy Technique

This type of therapy can be conducted in ways that include:

Parent-Child Sessions

These are common ones, and these are for a couple of reasons:

- To reconcile what the kid told the therapist on their behavior to see if they were being truthful but this without making the child feel as though they were doubting his words.
- To keep the parent updated on the progress of the kid
- To provide a platform for the kid and the parent to have an open heart to heart conversation
- To study the relationship between the kid and the parent and the effect it has on the kid.
- The parent also gets to be educated on parenting skills and how they affect the child

Family-Based Sessions

These sessions involve more than just the parents. The siblings, close friends, and family members are invited into these sessions. Here, a couple of things get to happen.

- The therapist gets their point of view on the condition
- How it affects them as individuals and their relationship with the kid
- They have been educated on an explosive disorder and sensitized over it
- Sometimes even the teacher is invited in this session for the therapist to see how they interact and advise them on the best way to go about things at school.

Group Sessions

These sessions involve the child, the therapist, and other children dealing with the same condition. Sometimes parents are allowed to attend these sessions, and other times it is just the therapist and the children discussing a behavioral disorder and the challenges they face in their daily lives, as well as how they deal with it all. This, in particular, helps children realize that they are not alone in their experiences and that they are free to discuss their concerns without fear of being judged by others.

Why Behavioral Therapy?

There are a few critical reasons why behavioral therapy should always be a part of explosive disorder treatment. To begin with, teens diagnosed with this disorder face daily problems that go well beyond their symptoms. Their inattentiveness, hyperactivity, and their impulsiveness only present one set of issues. There are additional problems that can appear as poor academic performance, misbehaving in school, or poor peer, sibling, and parental relationships. Your teen may disobey orders issued by adults and have other discipline problems.

Because they are predictors of how well your child will do in the long run, these problems are potentially serious, and you should not ignore them. Research indicates that how successful a child with the explosive disorder will be as an adult is best predicted by three factors:

1. The effectiveness of parent parenting skills
2. How well the child relates to other children
3. How well the child performs academically

There is no question that behavioral therapy effectively treats each of these domains. It instructs parents and teachers in methods that help them deal with an ADHD child. In the case of adolescents, it instructs them in helpful techniques for managing themselves. Once acquired, these skills can help the teen overcome their impairments. Because an explosive disorder is a chronic disorder, learning these skills is especially important. They will help a person diagnose it throughout their entire life.

Medication: The other component to treatment

is medication. Unfortunately, there is a myth that medication loses its effectiveness over time. There is no evidence to support this. However, with the hormonal changes that begin with puberty, a child's receptivity to a particular drug might change. As part of the diagnosis of your teen, a new evaluation of the medication should take place. Your child's maturation may mean they need to be switched to a different drug, or it may simply mean the dosage of their current drug should be increased.

Forms of Behavioral Therapy

Cognitive Behavioral Therapy, (CBT), is a therapeutic intervention that focuses on changing cognitive behaviors, improving emotional regulation, and developing coping strategies. Its focus is on behavior and helps children with disorder explosions learn organization skills, impulse control, and better way to manage their emotions.

Behavioral Therapy Techniques

When your child gets diagnosed with an explosive disorder, behavioral therapy is usually necessary. You still need to know what you should do to help your child when they are not in therapy by how you can improve their daily experience with helpful tips and tricks that many parents have been using for decades. These techniques are meant to give you an overall better understanding of how your child is feeling and what you can do to make their daily experiences less triggering. You will be able to recognize when your child is struggling because they will begin to act out or become hyperactive. These strategies will help you feel that you have more control of the situation. You can help your child and allow them to thrive in any environment. There are certain fundamentals of behavioral therapy for behavioral disorders in children, and they are easy to understand. Even without a medical professional by your side, you as a parent can do so much to help your child. Most of the time, it involves getting them out of the situation they are in that is causing them distress. What you must remember is that your child is not neurotypical. This means that situations that may seem mundane to you or other children might seem entirely different to your child—acceptance of this is the key.

These techniques can be used at any point by any parent. No matter how long your child has had their diagnosis, you can use these to assist you with difficult moments that usually seem impossible to get through. The thing about an explosive disorder is that it is fleeting. It reaches a peak, and then it simmers down if you know how to provide your child with the right coping skills. This is exactly what these techniques are designed for.

Make Sure Your Child Understands the Rules

Many parents lose their patience easily because they are often blind to the fact that a behavioral disorder prohibits children from being able to comprehend rules as easily as other children. Even if you have enforced them loud and clear, your child might still not get what you are expecting from them. You need to be certain that they understand the rules, and there are several ways for you to do this without having to punish them over and over. Telling your child what to avoid or giving subtle hints is not going to work.

Give Clear Commands

After you know that you have their attention, you can give them the command exactly as you want it performed. Do not leave anything up for interpretation because your child's brain is not going to know what to do with this information. For example, if you want them to take out the trash, you should tell them to take out the trash and put it in the bin outside. Then, you should tell them to replace the trash bag. This will avoid any confusion and any tasks that are only half-completed. You need to give clear directions in this way so that they can truly get what you are expecting from them. This is simply how your child's brain works, and there is nothing wrong with being direct.

Do Not Expect Perfection

There is no such thing as being perfect. Just as you will never be a perfect parent, there is never a moment when your child is going to behave perfectly. Perfection is a societal trap that makes you think you are not good enough and that you are not teaching your child enough. Instead of striving for perfection, recognize the circumstances. Notice when your child is doing the best that they can—given their circumstances. You must also recognize that you are doing the best you possibly can as a parent. This is good enough, and this should be enough to make you feel proud and accomplished. Perfection is so subjective because there are many ways that one can define the term. You might see perfection one way while someone else in your life sees it completely differently. Do not worry about reaching that state of ultimate perfection.

Adjust Your Rules as Your Child Gets Older

Your child is inevitably going to grow up quickly before your eyes. This means that you are going to have to make plenty of adjustments along the way, both with your parenting skills and the way that you discipline your child. The marble rewards system might become outdated as your child grows up, but you can still implement the same system verbally. Without focusing so much on points, you can simply state the consequences of their bad behavior as they relate to the fun activities your child wants to do. No matter how old your child gets, you are still going to be disciplining them as they live under your roof.

Strategies of Cognitive-Behavioral Therapy

Determine the Condition

The therapist will first ask you or the child to define the problem, the symptoms, and whether they could be caused by something other than the condition. They will inquire about your children's interactions with others at school, at home, and elsewhere. They will inquire as to how the child's condition affects their relationship with their peers.

Examine Thoughts, Behaviors, and Emotions That Are a Result of the Condition

They will then go over the symptoms in detail and how they affect the child's thoughts, behavior, and emotions. The therapist will examine how the child reacts when their condition reveals the severity of the symptoms. How do they affect emotions in turn, and how long do the episodes last?

Spot the Negative Thoughts, Behavior, and Emotions Brought about by the Condition

The child will be asked how they deal with all this when it happens. Do they choose to hide from others, or do they own up to the result of their actions? The parent is then asked to support the claim.

Work to Replace the Dark Thought, Behavior, and Emotions Brought about by the Condition

When the symptoms become too severe, the therapist and the child come up with alternatives to replace the reaction to the emotions they feel. They talk about what to do if they become aggressive. They are taught coping mechanisms as well as how to perceive situations. The therapist collaborates with the child and parent to develop solutions and alternatives.

CHAPTER 8

ADDITIONAL THERAPY TECHNIQUES

Parental Therapy

This therapy is for you, the parent. This form of treatment should be utilized in conjunction with the behavior therapy your child receives. Think of parental therapy as a type of parent training course. Every parent has wished at one time or another that their child came with a parenting handbook. Well, treatment for parents is going to serve as that handbook. It will teach you how to cope with your child's different behaviors. It is your chance to talk about how his/her actions affect you. You will talk about how you handle his/her behaviors, such as yelling too much or not being consistent with your expectations and consequences. The therapist is going to teach you how to respond to explosive disorder behaviors. Remember, your responses mean a lot to your child. They affect how he or she feels because your reactions, especially if they are negative, could tell him you might not like him/her.

During parental therapy, you will give you the mechanisms you desire to manage your child's behaviors at home. Teaching you how to change your parenting skills can be daunting and even a little insulting. However, you must keep an open mind because you cannot expect positive changes in your child without changing yourself for the better, too. Once you are equipped with the strategies and tools that you need to deal with explosive behaviors positively, you will start to see the changes reflected in your child. He or she will notice when you are no longer yelling at him/her for not listening but gently reminding him/her instead. These types of changes are quite impactful on the feelings of an explosive child.

Dialectical Conduct Therapy

Dialectical Behavior Therapy (DBT) is a type of therapy under the Cognitive Behavioral Therapy umbrella with the primary objective of teaching people how to cope healthily with stress, how to live in the moment, regulate their emotions as well as improve their relations with the people around them.

DBT was primarily intended for people with borderline personality disorder (BPD), and it has been adapted over the years to address other conditions patients have exhibited, such as eating disorders, self-destructive behaviors as well as substance abuse. DBT is also administered for patients with post-traumatic stress disorder.

Behavioral Modification

Therapists have been employing Behavior Modification treatments in the management of explosive disorders for the past three decades. These techniques have gained much respect over this period due to their experience and their curing for many children of aggressive and disruptive behavior. Children with behavioral disorders have learned to manage their actions and develop positive social skills and academic performance with these methods' help. Behavior Modification treatments for children with the explosive disorder could be divided into five categories:

1. Cognitive behavioral interventions
2. Clinical behavior therapy
3. Direct contingency management
4. Intensive behavioral treatments
5. Combination of behavioral and pharmacological treatments

Combination of Pharmacological and Behavioral Interventions

The combination of both medicinal and behavioral treatment has been useful for many children with explosive disorders in the past. It is more effective than either behavioral or medication treatment alone. If both medication and behavioral therapy are being used, therapists typically will decrease the times, doses, and medicines during behavioral sessions. However, note that decisions on the best use and combination of treatments will always depend on the individual patient.

Cognitive Behavioral Interventions

This method is commonly referred to as CBI. The goal of CBI is to focus on self-control through verbal self-instruction and problem-solving strategies, self-monitoring and evaluation, cognitive modeling, and other similar techniques. Your child will meet with a therapist once or twice a week to learn these strategies through methods such as role-play.

Therapists use a popular CBI technique that teaches a child to "stop" when he is disruptive. These self-instruction techniques have been introduced when children with disorders do not have the motivation to give themselves cues on what to do. Cognitive-behavioral interventions are becoming less popular as behavioral disorder experts focus on developing alternative techniques.

Contingency Management

This type of behavioral treatment, known as CM, follows a structured format and may include a special treatment classroom. The encouragement of actions through positive or negative reinforcement is one of the main principles used in CM. It entails using economic tokens as behavioral tools, such as the giving or withholding of rewards. Though most parents are used to using reward systems with their children, knowing the most effective methods of achieving results can be beneficial. After receiving CM treatment, your child will be better able to respond to your cues as well as the prohibitions and privileges you grant him.

Intensive Behavioral Treatments

It entails children, parents, and teachers to implement techniques that reward children for good behavior. The combination of methods aims to improve socialization, self-control, and academic abilities. Your child will attend school and perform better willingly by the end of intensive behavioral treatment.

Several intensive behavioral treatment summer camps are available, each lasting about eight weeks and perfectly timed before the school year. The typical mix of behavioral treatment and recreational activities at these camps ensures that the therapy is beneficial and enjoyable for the children.

Family Therapy

It is a therapy that is for the family. ADHD does not affect only the child; it affects the whole family. It is a disorder that is often disruptive to the family unit. The goal of family therapy is to help each member of your family cope with ADHD behaviors. The behaviors of your child affect each person differently. Family therapy will address each member of the family in private and as a group. It will teach each family member how to deal with their feelings about ADHD and how it has personally affected them.

That is an emotional form of talking therapy. Each session will give the entire family a chance to voice their feelings and concerns. Everyone is not expected to agree and everyone is not expected always to react the right way to ADHD behaviors. Family therapy can be quite emotionally-charged. Each person's feelings are valid, even negative emotions. Each session allows the family to talk to a neutral third-party. The therapist will listen to each concern and will help the family communicate with each other in constructive, positive ways.

CHAPTER 9
LIFE SKILLS YOUR CHILD NEEDS

Learning Self-Care

One of the first steps of dealing with explosive disorder is teaching your child how to care for themselves. As parents, you will be taking care of your child, but when your child knows how to take care of themselves, it is better than that because slowly, they will learn how to be self-reliant. And with that, children who have behavioral disorders also learn how to follow through and stay on track.

If you want your child to have the best self-care, you have to urge them to figure out what they want. When explosive children are not permitted to look after themselves or engage in self-care, they become even more exhausted, depressed, emotionally depleted, or even angry. When you teach your child how to put him or her on the top of their priority list, they will stop feeling overwhelmed and undeserving. Yes, at times, your teenage child might think that they will start looking after themselves once everything becomes okay, but that can become a far-fetched dream. You need to put yourself first now and teach your kids to do the same.

Practice Color-Coding

The strategy you can use to help your explosive child work on his/her organizational skills is color-coding. Indeed, those children will face some academic challenges, but that doesn't give them any excuse for giving up on stuff. Color coding is one such strategy that has always helped others who have explosive disorders to learn things quickly. You can separate the different subjects in your planner in different colors. That will help you understand stuff with just a single glance at your planner.

Helping Your Child Follow Through Independently

Helping your child do what they say they're going to do without having to remind them is vital. Scientists have built a way to help people with their plans to follow through. In this special way, if you help your child "planning for success," there is an increased chance that they will carry out their plan immediately on their own.

Ask your child to tell you what they're going to do and define when, where, and how they're going to do it as if they'd been rehearsing for a play. Then have them recognize the stimuli that will alert them to enforce their strategy in the area. You should step aside by making them focus on the setting to guide them. Since they take the lead, they are also expected to be better in their determination to follow through.

Developing Routines

Whenever we discuss the right way to bring up a child with a behavioral disorder, you will often come across the term structure. Do you know what it refers to? It is an environment that is more predictable and organized. To bring the form to your child's life, you have to create a schedule for them and make routines for their day-to-day life. Your child should clearly understand the consequences, expectations, and rules so that their environment is predictable. That, in turn, helps them in feeling secure. The ability to regulate themselves is something that explosive kids do not possess. They have so many distractions, and staying concentrated on any particular thing becomes impossible for them.

Exercising and Its Importance

It is no secret that exercise has several health advantages, but it can also help alleviate or even treat explosive symptoms in children and adults.

It is no secret that exercise has several health advantages, but it can also help alleviate or even treat behavioral symptoms in children and adults.

While no one knows what causes explosive disorder, evidence suggests it may be linked to a dopamine malfunction. It is stated that exercise not only promotes norepinephrine, dopamine, and serotonin synthesis in the brain, but it also has the same impact on the brain as that of the stimulant methylphenidate (Ritalin).

Exercise, then, is nature's antidepressant. Exercise-induced increases in dopamine can assist people with explosive disorders in improving their attention and concentration, but that is not all: Exercise also creates endorphins, the brain's "feel-good chemical." Exercise also aids in the release of restless energy, and that is a sign of explosibility in children and adults. Taking away a child's recess time is just the worst thing a trainer can do to them."

Meditation

According to research published, mindfulness meditation is beneficial in treating children with explosive disorders.

Mindfulness meditation, a technique in which an individual pays nonjudgmental attention to one's current experience, may be used to alleviate these symptoms.

Mindfulness is a two-step process that entails directing one's attention to a specific moment and then engaging that experience with curiosity and openness. This approach is an effective treatment for depression and anxiety in patients.

Encourage Good Hygiene

Children who are presently suffering from behavioral disorders face difficulties in doing even the simplest things in life, including maintaining proper hygiene. From the outside, it might feel that your child is not brushing teeth or taking a shower daily, but they think many things on the inside. Being a parent to a child having an explosive disorder is hard, but you have to take it one day at a time and take the baby steps necessary for teaching your child how to take care of their hygiene. Kids who have this disorder frequently get stuck in one particular thought, moment, or activity, and it takes them a lot of time to get done with something.

You might be telling your child a thousand times to shower or brush their teeth, and yet they keep forgetting because this is not how you should teach good personal hygiene values. If you are the person who is always telling them what to do and what not to do, then there will be a point of time where they will not be able to function until and unless you are present with them. Moreover, when you keep nagging with the same things, some children can hate it because it acts as a constant reminder that you doubt their abilities.

Mindfulness

Mindfulness (sometimes called Mindfulness-Based Cognitive Therapy) as a therapeutic technique is considered a new yet acceptable approach by clinicians in fending off depression, anxiety, ADHD, and various other health conditions. However, many psychologists face issues when attempting to utilize it as a treatment, largely because of the lack of formal training they received on the subject.

CHAPTER 10

Managing an Explosive Child Away From Home

Travelling can be hazardous. If your child goes beyond the bounds and causes damage to the property of others, the consequences could be costly. Even if you do not limit your child's explosive behavior, you risk failing to complete errands and upsetting strangers. It would be fine if self-managed, so how can you make that happen?

As a parent, you are going to need to come up with several different plans of action for your child. These plans will help them with any struggles or difficulties they encounter because of their disorder symptoms. Whether they are having an outburst at home or a complete meltdown in public, you need to prepare yourself for the possibility that anything can happen at any moment in time. If one thing is for certain, it is that there is nothing certain about the explosive disorder. Your child will also not necessarily be able to tell you when something is about to happen, so you need to pay close attention to their cues.

Weekends and Vacations

Establishing a schedule for weekends and vacations when the school routine is out is also extremely important. It would ease if you still organized regular hours for eating, medications, therapy, sleep, and play. Special classes can be inserted into the routine if needed. Outdoor activities, like hiking or camping, are excellent. During school vacations, don't merely tag your child with errands or allow him/her to sit bored while you work; that will only make his/her symptoms worse.

It may not be advisable to take your child to theme parks or museums. Children can act up in museums, especially if they're not designed for young minds. Those where you can only see but not touch will bring out your child's negative symptoms.

On the other hand, amusement parks are generally over-stimulating because of the arousing decorations, lights, and sounds. They are designed to stir the emotions and senses, which is not incredibly healthy for your child. However, some amusement parks, like Disneyland and Knott's Berry Farm, allow special passes for kids with behavioral disorders. These parks treat such children sensitively, ensuring they don't need to wait in line just to reach the rides.

Holidays and Events

When your child begins to socialize at school with other kids, he or she will begin to receive invitations, such as birthday parties, and it is right that they should attend. Just remember that any particular event involving your child can raise both their excitement and anxieties, so you must prepare ahead. For a child with a behavioral disorder, Christmas Eve is as important an occasion as a visit to the dentist, and you should plan to calm their expectations or fears of the day.

When your own child's party, you should keep it low-key. You don't need to compete in the biggest party contests, as some parents do at this age. Just invite your child's closest friends and take them out for ice cream. Nor should you allow yourself to get stressed by the annual holiday seasons. You don't have to hang up as many lights and decorations as your neighbors. Just stick to the essential family rituals, like a special dinner and opening presents together.

Tips for Traveling with Young Children

Going with adolescents over an all-encompassing timeframe requires more than basically the acquisition of modest plane tickets and rebate lodgings. This is especially valid if the get-away goal will be new to everybody voyaging.

Guardians should be prepared to manage the unforeseen. Additional tolerance and a comical inclination are musts on any outing with minimal ones. Cleverness can defuse numerous upsetting circumstances.

Coming up next are tips that help make a family get-away a triumph:

- Pack sound tidbits. You don't need your little ones to eat treats before flying since sugar can build a child's anxiety, fractiousness, and disturb rest schedules.

- Allow enough time for several restroom visits preceding loading up.
- Bring exercises to kill time. Tablets and shading books can demonstrate to give valuable interruptions.
- When boarding, urge your children to locate their seats.
- Stress the significance of keeping their safety belts clasped.
- If this is your child's first flight, depict how taking off will feel before loading up and clarify how at some point flights hit choppiness.
- Try to remain at a lodging that offers free Continental breakfast. This sets aside cash and time and eases the heat off finding an eatery every morning.
- Find a neighborhood supermarket so you can buy your child's recognizable snacks for day trips and lodging.
- Map out where you will be venturing out in front of time.

Traveling with Your Explosive Child

The new relationship you develop with your child will be highly beneficial wherever you go, but specific unusual issues may arise during car rides. Driving when your child is misbehaving is both aggravating and dangerous. You may be in a hurry at times, and if your child refuses to assist, they will ruin everything.

You want your child to put on a seat belt without prompting, but they may refuse if upset about something else. It makes more sense to investigate the source of the child's annoyance rather than focusing solely on lack of compliance. Because the back seat can be lonely, being proactive can help you avoid unwanted attention. You can include your child in a conversation, pack items of interest, or play a game with them to make the trip less lonely and boring.

You may be concerned about your child's health if he or she causes a commotion while driving. You may need to find a safe place to park the car and wait for it to calm down. Yes, you may be late, but it is your best option. "Seeing more than one child ride with you is safe only to drive if we sit in our seats and get along," tell your child. However, when you return to the lane, make sure the kids stop fighting and do something else, even if it's just looking out the window. Fighting can resume fast if they are not distracted from the conflict.

When there is constant disagreement over the seating arrangement in the car, apply the same techniques that you would use to minimize conflict within the household; help the kids figure out the sharing system they want to use. Do this before your next trip; ask the kids if they have any suggestions to fix the problem when everyone is calm. Every child may have a unique seating choice, but as long as the kids find out what works for them, everything will be fine. Ensure that their program correctly informs them, or it is unlikely to be effective, who has first preference at specific times. You should not keep track of whose turn it is for the seat they want.

Problems in the Store

Your child may be very cooperative if you are looking for something they enjoy. However, when they feel compelled to buy for others, their actions may be markedly different. As is often the case, when they lack the authority to decide what happens, your child's explosive behavior is sparked and intensified.

If you're in a good mood, your child will behave better, so you have a lot of power. Talking about your child's favorite topics of conversation can also help make unnecessary shopping less annoying. Most importantly, if your child understands what is going on, he or she is more likely to comply. For example, if you're going grocery shopping, you could ask her if she wants to help you decide what to buy. Older children may be willing to assist you in your search for bargains. Others may wish to read the grocery list or push the cart.

Public Misbehavior

Unfortunately, if your behavior becomes disrespectful or dangerous, you may be forced to stop your child or leave the store physically. In some cases, you may be able to re-enter the store after a short time if your child calms down and you are confident that everything will be fine when you return.

However, you might have to return. Your child must understand that their actions have repercussions. In these circumstances, you can demonstrate such negative consequences. To begin, "Because we haven't finished our shopping, we'll have to return later, and I won't be able to make the dessert I was planning for tonight." If the problem persists, you may want to take it a step further. You could suggest that your child use some of their own money to pay for the return trip, emphasizing the benefits of this option (e.g., this compensates others for inconveniencing them) and might mitigate their complicated feelings against them). Everyone benefits when they offer reimbursement.

As with hygiene issues, you could also ask your child if they want to stay home the next time and use some of their own money to hire someone to keep their company. As a result, they bear some of the burdens of refusing to comply with the family plan. Offer them options, but let them know that some of them may come at a cost.

Relationship with non-family members

Is your child accusing other children of gaining a sense of superiority? Is attempting to "buy" friends by giving away personal items while demonstrating low self-esteem? Should he complain about being mistreated to get you to run her defense? Will he always sit alone on the playground, or will he only play with kids outside the standard circle? Please consider changing it. You want your child to have a fun social life and to feel comfortable interacting with a wide range of people.

When he meets another rambunctious child, his behavior frequently becomes exaggerated as a child with explosive disorder. If he behaves stupidly and doesn't try to meet standards, he stops feeling inferior, and there is no loss when he plays with another cap tester. There is strength in numbers, and when your child joins forces with a "bad friend," he gains influence and leverage.

You can try to keep your child away from other disruptive children. However, it may give your child the impression that he or she is weak and easily manipulated. Another approach is to help them understand why they are incorrect and assist them in successfully dealing with negative influences. This approach gives them the impression that they will show up and affect change in their environment. They will regard themselves as a wise leader. "Your friend might be clever enough to imitate you when you're playing together," you might say.

If your child is young, he will most likely mimic many of the behaviors he observes in other adults in the family. If he is demanding and possessive with you, he may also be challenging and possessive with his playmates. When family members manipulate or disrespect him or mistreat him, he may overreact or exhibit fear. For these reasons, it is critical to cultivating habits that are compatible with non-family members. Improve his ability to connect within the group if you want him to communicate, accept social boundaries, and interact assertively with his peers.

Exercise

Most forms of exercise help to sharpen attention, promote learning, and improve social skills. Encourage your children to exercise. Let them go swimming, biking, or jogging. Let them dance, run, or play soccer. Take them backpacking so they can enjoy the beauty of nature.

Children benefit in varied ways when they engage in regular exercise. They interact with other children. They have fun. They stay healthy. They have self-confidence.

Aside from providing these benefits, regular exercise generates other effects that have a positive impact on a child who has disorder explosions.

A child with explosive disorder is impulsive, unfocused, or hyperactive. They are edgy and fidgety. They seem to be in perpetual motion; they chatter incessantly, squirm, run around, and are generally restless and unfocused.

Exercise helps control these symptoms. It helps a child harness his energy. It gives him a target, something to focus their energy and attention on. It helps them stay focused and motivated.

Exercise controls aggression. It provides an outlet for excess energy. It helps improve your child's mood. It makes them less anxious and less cranky throughout the day.

Exercise also helps your child sleep better at night. A healthy level of physical exhaustion induces deep sleep which is beneficial for your child.

CHAPTER 11
IMPROVING SOCIAL SKILLS OF EXPLOSIVE CHILDREN

How to Identify Challenges in Social Skills

According to research, children with explosive disorder explosions have social problems such as strained relationships with their classmates, trouble establishing and retaining friends, and deficits in proper social conduct. Long-term outcome studies show that these issues persist into adolescence and adulthood, obstructing individuals with this disorder social adjustment.

Suggestions for spotting challenges:

- Look around you for hints to assist you in interpreting the subtext. Keep an eye out for more alternatives. Keep your eyes peeled.
- To better understand what someone is saying, pay attention to their tone of voice, body language, demeanor, or the expression in their eyes.
- To better discern the subtext, look at a person's choice of words. ("I would love to go" is most likely a yes.) "If you want to" implies that you probably won't, but I will do it anyhow.)

Words are less effective than actions. If someone's words indicate one thing, but their actions suggest another, it is a good idea to think about if their actions reflect their actual sentiments.

Being bullied, or witnessing bullying; being overly aggressive with other children or classmates; winning or losing at play; not being able to handle the equipment; not wanting to play with other children; more risks on playground equipment.

Explosive children very often may have problems with rules and socialization, with their peers at school (during breaks in particular), or on the playground.

Below are some common situations and suggestions to help children deal with them.

Children with behavioral disorders unfortunately because of their being "clumsy" and impulsive, can be the target of a well-known social scourge called bullying.

Mind you, bullying is different from teasing because it is a repeated act, it is a subversive system that often escalates over time. It can include name-calling, threats, exclusion, and even physical violence.

Therefore, how to help?

First and foremost, talk about it: explain well what bullying is and make sure the child knows they can talk to their parent, or teacher about it if they experience it, or see it.

Explain that he will do well to leave if he doesn't feel

safe, or if using words to defend himself doesn't work, indeed responding with insults to other insults can throw gasoline on the fire.

Being Overly Aggressive with Other Children or Classmates

Explosive children sometimes totally lack impulse control and have trouble filtering what they say. They may physically push other children simply because they dislike something about them, run around inattentively, or call names.

It is also possible that they may not realize their strength.

So, what needs to be done?

It is critical to set and explain the ground rules well at home to avoid physical aggression so that the child knows the consequences beforehand. Encourage using words instead of one's body to communicate.

Before entering the park, for example, it's helpful to remind your child that being hit, or wounded, can hurt a lot...but also the importance of asking with words before taking, waiting your turn, and apologizing.

Often it is not enough for them to explain it with words alone, you have to simulate some situations at home and repeat them together, to make sure they have understood (role play).

Not Wanting to Play with Other Children

Being on the playground involves learning social skills explosive children lack, including sharing, taking turns, and knowing how to converse.

The child may not be sure how to start a conversation, fit into a small group of other children, or how to ask to participate in a game. He or she may not understand when other children are inviting him or her to play. This can make it difficult to develop friendships.

How to help them make distinctions?

Again, practice this at home. It is very useful to simulate introductions, suggesting some examples: "Hello, I'm Paolo, what's your name?" or perhaps: "Would you like to play ball with me?" "Please, may I join you?"

It will be important to explain to the child that sometimes it is not possible to participate in a game that is already in progress and organized without asking explicitly how to do it (simulation), which is not obvious to him.

Effect of Explosive Disorder on Peer Relationships

When a child hosts a birthday party and none of the children who were invited show up, it is upsetting not only for the child but also for the parent. Parents want to see their children laughing and having fun with their peers, and it is never easy when they are isolated.

It is not like children do not want to make friends; they do, but they just do not know how to do it. Sometimes it is not always the other children's fault that they will not associate with your child, but their parents may have a hand in that. For example, teens who have no sense of danger may persuade their peers to skip school. The parent of the child who does not have the condition will undoubtedly warn their adolescent to stay away from the "troubled child." There are numerous things a parent can do to prevent this from happening. However, before that, parents must understand how explosive affects the child's relationship with their peers.

Express Impatience by Not Waiting Their Turn

Explosive children are very impatient as has been proven in previous cases. It does not exactly bond well with your peers if you keep cutting them in line. Children are impatient tiny people, but they are trained to practice the art. A child with a behavioral disorder does not have the sense to be patient and will find themselves cutting others in the line. Assume that a child has been waiting in line for sweets when another child cuts them in line and ends up getting the candy; when it is their turn, their candy is gone. Of course, the child will not blame the adult for not bringing enough candy but will remember that the reason they did not get one was because of another child who couldn't wait as long as they could.

This resentment from the children is unlikely to encourage them to befriend the child with the explosive disorder. It is even more difficult to persuade them that it was not the child's fault. How do you explain to a group of 12-year-olds that the behavioral child explosions did not cause the mishap on purpose when they witnessed it? While you can explain away a behavior to other adults and have them understand, this is not the same case with children. So, in this case, it is the explosive child that needs guidance. You will need to talk to them and guide them on how to approach certain situations, so they don't end up annoying and hurting their peer's feelings, and, thus developing a negative reputation among them.

Talk Over Their Peers

Explosive children battle with concentration. They talking over others is viewed as a sign of disrespect, and other children do not take too kindly to it. Sometimes, those children do this to keep their focus on the conversation as they have a very short attention span. Talking and listening need active participation, and it is easier for those children to talk than to listen. This is because their short attention span does not allow them to stay focused on the same thing for a long time.

Have a Difficult Time Paying Attention to Others

This comes back to them having a short attention span. Imagine having a conversation with someone, sharing something with them only to find they are not paying attention to you. And to make it worse, they missed almost the whole conversation. This is going to, without a doubt, make you angry—especially when you listen when it is their turn, and the least, they can do for you is pay attention.

Unlike teens who also encounter this problem, they do not exactly understand that this is an effect of a condition. Explaining this to a child may be difficult, and besides, it is the child with the condition who requires assistance because a parent will not always be present in all their child's interactions to explain away the behavior.

Get Jealous of the Other Children

When the child wants to make friends, this is not the right attitude to have. If they are in art class working on something that needs all their focus, this child will grow resentful that the other children remained focused on their work, enough to finish it on time and receive commendation from the teacher. They can't be friends if they hate the other person for things that are beyond their control.

Parents must understand that if they do not help their children acknowledge and accept their situation, first and foremost by leading by example, the child will grow to despise what they are and those who have what is beyond their means. Being envious of other children can be relatively harmless, but it must be stopped before it becomes so.

Like to Be the Center of Attention

Explosive children who are hyperactive frequently perform dangerous stunts to impress their peers. It is sometimes necessary to make a statement such as, "Look, I can do this better than you." As a way of proving themselves and making amends for their shortcomings. For example, a student may be having difficulty focusing on a class assignment, and the teacher continues to call them out in front of the entire class, embarrassing them. This child will feel the need to draw attention to themselves and distance themselves from the other thing they are unable to do. That thing on which the other kids are fixated. They may play dangerous pranks on other students or get into fights over trivial matters to demonstrate to you that they are more than that one thing they can't do and that what they can do, they can do better than you.

Parents Role in Helping Their Children Make Friends

Explosive children may appear insensitive to the feelings of others, unsure of what to say or how to act when confronted with situations in which their response is expected, and not just any response, but one that has a positive impact. It is not enough to simply tell the child how to behave; you must also demonstrate how to do so. Here is how you can do it.

Say your child had a conversation with their peer at school where the other kid was talking about how they were having problems with a math assignment. Just a simple conversation, however, it goes on longer than it usually would because the other kid breaks out into details of the work. This is already enough to have the explosive child grow bored. As far as we know about behavioral disorders, we realize two things might happen in this particular case. Those children may interrupt the conversation and bring up a whole different topic and thus make the other feel dismissed, or the child will just zone off and start daydreaming which has the same result as the first.

Control the Environment

Picking a safe environment for your child, whether they have an explosive disorder or not is very important. Look at the place you are taking your child to study and play with other children. The daycare that you take your child off to. Are they in an environment surrounded by people that are sensitive to mental health issues or are they willing to learn and adjust accordingly?

What parents need to understand is that the environment in which you send your kid is very important because this influences them. The people around you can help or hurt your child's mental health. For example, a school where children learn about mental health and how it affects others. When your child is zoning out during a conversation, they do not take it personally and do everything they can to refocus their attention on the topic at hand. This is not to say that the children must like or tolerate when explosion symptoms manifest in situations, but they understand and are unwilling to let it affect their relationship with the child.

Be an Example

Children learn by example. What you do is what they'll find themselves doing and that's why sometimes people use the words, "You take after your mother" or "Your father would have done the same thing." All this starts at a pretty young age and the habits stick into their teenage years that follow them into adulthood.

When it comes to friends—the kind you have, how you treat them, and they treat you, in turn, does not go unnoticed to the child. Do you sit around and talk about that friend who is not around, say mean things about them, and then pretend all that did not happen when they come? Do you go to them when they are in trouble and do they come to your aid when something goes wrong on your end?

Sign Them Up for Social Groups

This is where you assist your child. Children with explosive disorder thrive in social settings, as opposed to children with depression or social anxiety who prefer it when left to their own devices. It's not that they don't want to make friends; they just don't know how to do it. How do they get these kids to like them and want to hang out with them?

This not only helps them make friends, but it also teaches them new skills. Assume you sign them up for a music class in which they must collaborate with other children. Playing a musical instrument requires concentration, but it is also a changing and repetitive activity. Repetitiveness is beneficial because it allows them to become experts in one area and provides a pattern for them to follow. Because they will not always play the same thing all the time, the art remains interesting.

Keep In Contact with Their Caregivers

Parents with explosive children need to keep in contact with their caregivers or teachers. When the child's babysitter understands the child's condition, they get in a better position to help the child. Assume that the teacher at your children's school understands the child's condition and recognizes that they lose focus in class, making it difficult for them to focus on their work; they also recognize that the child has learning difficulties. They will not address the children's issues in front of the rest of the class, which will embarrass them.

Arrange Playdates for the Children

Invite your friend's children over and arrange playdates. Most of the time, family friends run in families where the children are friends because their parents are friends. What better person is there than the one who has been with you and does not require you to explain your child's condition because they have been there the entire journey? By extension, their child comprehends the situation. Playdates with other children and encouraging sleepovers help the children bond.

When parents and children spend time together, they form bonds. For example, when you organize play dates for your child, they can share and discover what they have in common, allowing the conversations to be light and the child not to have to try too hard.

Ease Your Kid into Social Settings

Explosive children already have self-esteem issues and are afraid of others' rejection because of what they already know. Using the previous example, where the children in their class are already aware that this child has learning difficulties, their self-esteem is already crushed, how do you as a parent ease your child into the social setting, especially when they are reluctant to do so? Easing a child into a social setting mostly entails the step you take before you let them interact with others and they may include:

Talk about the Issues You Encounter When Presented with a Situation like Theirs

Help them understand that there is no such thing as a perfect friend and tell them the challenges you encountered when it came to making friends in their age and ways in which you encounter the issues to date. This way, they won't feel so bad about themselves when it doesn't work out in the long run. They will understand that sometimes friendships work and sometimes they just don't.

In a social setting, parents should refrain from speaking for their children because you are not assisting them. You must remember that you will not always be with that child. Trying to explain their condition instead of allowing the child to try on their own is not helping them. You must allow them to make mistakes for them not to repeat them.

How to Help Your Child Make Friends

- **Congratulate them.** When they do have successful interactions, congratulate your child. Watch them closely when they play with other kids so you can always keep a watchful eye and monitor the situation; they are in. You can intervene if there is a fight if your child starts telling fibs or if they are trying to attempt something dangerous to impress their friends.
- **Try not to dive in.** When introducing a new sport

to your explosive child, speak with the coach first before going in for the first practice. Ask questions about whether your child who has the explosive disorder is welcomed in the team. You can follow your child to meet the instructor, who may introduce your child to the game a little bit before the first practice.

- **Take note of their competitive attitude explosive children can also have difficulty in competitive play.** Gloating on winning and crying on losing. If your child experiences these circumstances with difficulty, get them to learn other kinds of athletic abilities that do not require doing it as a team, such as martial arts, running, gymnastics, golfing, and cycling.

- **Trust that they will find their way.** Children will eventually learn to cope and handle their situations and behaviors better, even when they have experienced social isolation. They will also learn how friendships work. When a child hits adolescence, they will act on the urge to fit in.

- **Having just a few friends.** This is something that needs to be drilled into the child. They do not need to be part of a huge group of friends or be invited into plenty of parties to be happy. Studies show that having close friends is what is needed for a child to be happy, to be socially developed, and to have self-confidence.

- **Find a mentor.** Having a peer who acts as a big brother or big sister can be extremely helpful as they are more likely to take advice or instructions from them than from a parent. You can ask an elder sibling to become an informal mentor to your child. Many schools offer mentorship programs so you can ask your school if they can connect your child to a peer.

- **Follow the love.** Your child may already be interested in a certain sport or a video game. If they already have developed an interest in a specific game or skill, help them connect with an interest group as this will help your child feel confident, engaged, and belong.

- **One-on-one play.** Playdates with one child can prove to be extremely helpful for children to learn social cues. You can add on two children to the playdate, but more than that may seem overwhelming, and your disorder explosions child may like they are being attacked.

- **Set good examples.** Teaching your child the best ways to react and act in social situations, will help them make that same determination to form and create friendships with the children of your friends too.

- **Take teasing head-on bullying, playful banter and teasing are all the inevitable elements of childhood and friendships.** Explosive children may not be able to respond correctly, so parents are advised to help the child maneuver through the teasing and harassment they face by standing up to their bullies, not overreacting, and seeking out an adult's help at any time.

- **Keep playdates short.** For children aged 10 or

under, it's probably best for playtime to be less.

- **Getting the dosage right.** Puberty is a good period to relook the dosage and medication given to your child. As puberty hits, your child will go through all sorts of hormone changes in their body. Often things that worked before puberty may not have the same effect anymore.

- **Observe your child.** When they are playing with other children, sit back and observe. You can learn a lot about how your child socializes if you just watch how they play. Pay attention to when they get frustrated and what sets them off. Most of the time, explosive children are a lot more prone to frustration and having outbursts than the average child. Try not to insert yourself too much.

- **Believe they will find their way.** You need to let your child make mistakes and do what they feel is instinctually right. Even if they mess up, they are learning. As long as they are not hurting themselves or anyone else, you need to step back to allow them to grow.

Helping Your Child Improve Their Social Skills

Simple social interactions prove to be another hurdle for explosive children. These difficulties are such as talking too much or not being able to read social cues, interrupting frequently, or just coming off as too intense or aggressive. Because they mature differently from their peers, those children can be a subject of teasing and bullying. Despite their emotional immaturity, they are gifted with an acute sense of creativity and intelligence. Often, they figure out ways of coping or getting along with other children or even spot people who are not friends. Their personality traits can sometimes exasperate parents as well as teachers, but sometimes to their peers, it can be funny and charming.

Social skills and rules can be a hurdle for explosive disorder children. In this area, you can help them become better listeners or even become better at reading people's faces and body language when they interact with their peers.

Show them how to make changes with their behavior by speaking gently and honestly to them about their challenges.

Help your child through various scenarios by doing some role-play to make learning social skills fun. Choose playmates that have similar abilities and language capacities as your child, so they do not feel out of place.

At first, invite just one or two friends. Pay attention while they are playing and have a policy of zero tolerance to hit, push and scream.

During a child's development phase, some skills are quantifiable language skills, math skills, etc.

But what about the softer skills which, like social skills, do not come as naturally? Explosive kids also find it difficult to make friends and establish relationships. Some parents wonder how social skills can be developed, but often don't know where to start.

All kids must have positive peer relationships and friendships. However, most explosive children have a hard time making friends and being included in a wider group of peers. Oftentimes, hyperactivity, inattention as well as impulsiveness can disrupt a child's attempt at connecting with the people around them positively. Not feeling belonging, not being accepted, feeling different, isolated, and unlikeable is, unfortunately, the painful feelings explosive children go through, and this experience carries on into adulthood, often with lasting and disastrous effects on their future attempts at making friends and forming connections. Explosive children are no different than children without all of them wanting to be liked, want to be part of a group, and want to make friends, they just do not know how to do it.

Increasing a Child's Social Awareness

According to various researches on explosive disorders, children with this condition can be low monitors of their social behavior. They often do not have clarity on the awareness or understanding of social situations and the reactions they provoke from people around them. To them, a peer interaction went well, but, or to the other person; it did not.

An explosive child's interaction with a peer may have gone well, but it did not. It is another example of a disorder explosions-related issue. According to the social setting, they cannot accurately "read" social situations, self-monitor themselves, and adjust their actions and behaviors. These skills would need to be taught directly to them.

Teach Skills Directly and Practice, Practice, Practice

Learning from past experiences also makes it a little more challenging when it comes to explosive children. They often react without thinking, but one way to remedy this would be to continually provide feedback immediately whenever a child's behavior is inappropriate or has had social miscues. Role-play is a beneficial way of shaping, teaching, and practicing positive social skills and providing the child with ways to deal with difficult situations, such as bullying and teasing.

CHAPTER 12

Explosive Child at School. Principles of Behavioral Management Technique at School

Impact of Explosive Disorder on Education

It is common to have an educational and learning impact with the explosive disorder. The classroom is another area where those explosions can be detected, and when brought to the doctor's attention, it can provide a more accurate diagnosis for the child, apart from what the parent has observed at home. When it comes to the classroom, challenges faced by the growing child include learning impairments and restrictions that affect their academic ability. Other issues that could show up are also limited reading capabilities, limited calculating and writing skills as well as sequencing movements. The child could also have trouble doing general tasks, they can also have interpersonal issues relating to their peers, playing with their peers, and having an interpersonal issue with friends and authoritative figures.

Academic and education problems are often the signs recorded in research and studies of explosive children. While the symptoms such as impulsivity, lack of concentration, hyperactivity as well as intermittent aggression are less severe, it is still to a high degree when compared to children without the behavioral disorder.

These studies also show that when these children come into adulthood, they fall into these main groups:

- Most of these children have limitations in learning

and applying their skills and knowledge
- They have sustained functional impairment
- They also have constrained social participation
- They have restricted social involvement
- In the end, around 25% work in parallel with those without ADHD
- Less than 25% of adults end up developing substantial problems.
- To date, it is unclear what factors contribute to the long-term outcomes of disorder explosions.

Choosing a School for Explosive Child

For students, behavioral disorders may be a challenging issue. It impacts a child's capacity to focus, concentrate, and give their all in academics. If a youngster is hyperactive, he or she may find it difficult to sit still, becoming restless and uncomfortable in the process. Some children cannot resist their need to speak at inopportune moments, interrupting the learning process for the rest of the class.

Despite the difficulties, schools may develop programs and processes to reduce distractions and assist these children in focusing on their work.

Here are 6 pointers to help you choose the appropriate school and programs.

1. Find out more about your child's learning preferences.

Before you select any school, you must first understand your child's personality and academic problems. Here are a few questions to ponder.

- Is it easier for them to learn or recall things if they can touch them?
- Is it true that your youngster learns best when they are moving?

2. Take note of the structure. Explosive students require daily organization and consistency. Because there are defined expectations and processes, this framework can serve as a basis for learning. It enables pupils to focus on a single piece of information simultaneously instead of a string of data.

3. Determine the student-teacher ratio. The average student-to-teacher ratio is 16 to 1. The school you pick should, at the very least, mirror the national average. However, when it comes to explosive pupils, the smaller the ratio, the better.

4. Many parents might feel their responsibilities end at home with the kid, and that the teacher is who should deal with them at school. However, parents play a bigger role in their child's school lives than just dropping them at school and attending PTA meetings once a month. Admittedly, teachers do play a very big role in the child's life, especially differently-abled ones.

5. Work with the child's teachers and others to help your child control the disorder and get as much from the school experience as possible. Allowing your child to perform well at school is a big part

of coping with behavioral disorders in children. For your child to flourish at school, there must be a collaboration between the teachers, school administrators, and the child's parents. Teachers should be well-informed about the child's condition so everyone can be on the same page regarding his needs.

6. It is also essential to let the teachers and school officials know that you have expectations for your child as far as his education is concerned. Make it clear what your goals and objectives are and work with them to achieve them. Get input from the teachers regarding how reasonable those expectations are and welcome their advice and recommendations but be alert for signs that the school has given up on your child and speak to the teachers about it right away. If both teams are not working in tandem, the child will not flourish in that atmosphere.

Teaching an Explosive Student

You may be wondering if your child's teacher is doing all that they can to support your explosive child's learning journey this is a common concern. Plenty of parents may be wondering it can be both hard for a teacher and a parent, and often, the collaboration between parent & teacher can determine the success of the child's coping skills at home and in school as well as their success in life. After parents, teachers play a very important role in the student's life and when behavioral disorder strategies are employed in a classroom setting, this can demonstrate to the child that they are worthwhile and capable, the child will believe this, and positive results will follow through.

You may be a parent reading this to know what a teacher can do in school, or you may be a teacher exploring ways to help the explosive student in class whatever it may be, here are some effective strategies that can guide both parent and teacher to establish a structured and supportive classroom inclusive one, encourages learning, enforces discipline and boosts self-esteem.

Making Rules and Routines Are a Part of an Explosive Student's Life

It is just not at home that rules and routines are important. Set short, simple rules in the classroom with student feedback. Again, positive reinforcements and feedback are essential. Instead of saying NO, you cannot do this, or NO you cannot do that, give students an outlet, or a template of what is expected of them. You can say "When you get into a class, check the board for your assignments before you do anything else" or you can say "When you enter class, speak only when you have settled in your desk." Your instructions could also be "Find your seats first and then you may talk quietly with your friend. When I start teaching, the conversations need to stop."

Establish Classroom Sequences

Doing so will help stay on task for explosive students. Some of these routines include having Row Captains that are in charge of making assignments is collected at the end of the day. You can also make it a point for explosive students to check in with the teacher or with a peer or Row Captains to see if the assignment is understood and if there's anything that they may need to clarify.

Give Appropriate Supervision to Explosive Students

We need to make one thing clear; explosive disorder is not a learning disability, like dyslexia, for example. This disorder makes learning difficult. It just makes it hard to learn something when a student struggles with focus and concentration and to focus on what the teacher is saying, and when they also cannot sit down and pay attention.

School Options for Children with the Explosive Disorder

The explosive disorder gets solved through learning. You can't absorb information or get work done if you're experimenting with the classroom or zoning out of your immediate environment.

Understand what the school requires children to do; sit

down; listen; concentrate; adhere to instructions; focus. They are things explosive children have trouble doing, not because they aren't prepared, but because their brains won't let them. But that doesn't mean that those kids can't do well in school.

There are several things parents and educators can do to help explosive children thrive in class. It begins with analyzing each child's weaknesses and talents, then discovering creative techniques to help a child focus, stick to a task, and work out how to explore their full potential.

Relationship between Explosive Disorder and Learning Disabilities

When we learn, our brain involves various executive functions, especially the elements that concern paying attention, focusing, engaging in a task, and using working memory. Through research, we also know that explosive disorder affects the brain's executive functions. For many people struggling with a behavioral disorder, learning, and schoolwork are a challenge because it involves these executive functions, but they do not have enough of an impairment to be diagnosed with LD. Suppose a person has signs of explosive disorder and LD together. In that case, this means that he or she has significant impairment in executive functions along with the loss of the specific skills required for reading, writing, and mathematics.

Expose Explosive Children to High-Interest Literature

One of the best ways to help an explosive child who struggles to read is to give them books on subjects that interest them. Some children like dinosaurs or trains; they may like elephants or even unicorns, pandas, Peppa Pig, or fairy tales. Giving children books related to the topics that interest them can help them do a better job recalling the text they read. You can teach your students how to become active readers by also teaching them various literacy strategies. For those students, maintaining attention to stories and passages that are stimulating, exciting, and shorter has a higher success rate.

Teach Active Reading Strategies

Active reading strategies can be taught to your students and even those with reading difficulties. These strategies are:

- Underlining texts and words.
- Taking and adding little notes to words that are hard to pronounce.
- Using colored pencils to mark syllables.
- Using highlighters to highlight new words.
- Post it to jot down important points to remember.
- Using colors to highlight phrases and passages.
- We are using icons like stars and circles.

If the student cannot write tips and notes in the book, the parent can get a second-hand copy of the book or, if allowed, make a copy of the book so the student can highlight, make notes, underline, circle, and write on their reading material.

As an educator, you can walk the student through this reading process and explain to them the various strategies they can use, how vital highlighting is, and how to make sense of the words together. This guided practice should be done at all reading sessions to develop students' competence with "Active Reading" skills.

Preview Content to Improve Reading Comprehension

You are previewing materials before reading and it is always a good idea for explosive students and even students with dyslexia. Both teacher and student can list essential information in the reading material, which appears on the passages. As a teacher, you can also provide general information about the reading topic, the characters, and the setting to give the students some head start.

Before the student reads a passage, follow him/her through several summary techniques by looking at the title, headings, diagrams, bold or italicized words, sidebars, and questions. You can also discuss how the reading material is arranged in its sequence.

Provide students with instruction in finding introductory and summary paragraphs. Using story maps or mind maps to help students recognize the main components of reading material and arrange them is also an ideal way to make reading easier.

Reading Aloud, in Silence

The subvocalizing technique is also an excellent tool for reading. In contrast to silent reading, it means speaking words while you read aloud but softly. The point here is to subvocalize as if you are reading it aloud, but just reading it softly. In other words, other students are not able to hear it. Reading aloud is a great strategy buff for some; it just slows the reading process. Silent reading can be difficult for children with problems with attention. The input from subvocalizing often helps these students to concentrate on the text.

Use Monitoring Methods

Teaching students techniques for monitoring their reading comprehension is also a great way to improve reading. Getting them to practice paraphrasing, summarizing paragraphs, asking questions, and even making predictions about what may happen in the story are all part of monitoring. It also helps create better clarity on the reading material.

Allocating More Time to Read

As with dyslexia, they are giving disorder explosions students extended time for reading and it is beneficial. For many students, their main issue is working memory and slower processing of information speed. So, they would greatly benefit when additional time is given to read and comprehend their reading materials. Not only that, but the extra time also gives students enough opportunity to process the reading materials effectively. The extended time helps the student to interpret the content effectively. They can look back, correct those misunderstandings and mistakes, seek explanations, and reread the text for a more extended period.

CHAPTER 13

STRATEGIES FOR EXPLOSIVE CHILD TREATMENT AT SCHOOL

Explosive Disorder and School

Every child has the right to have a proper education, regardless of gender, race, religious beliefs, or disabilities. An explosive child s is no different than any other child when it comes to understanding things around him or her. Getting diagnosed does not mean a child has a low IQ. There are many people with a high intelligence quotient who have explosive disorders. Any parent wants their child to have the best education possible, probably more so for parents of children who have special needs. The first thing to consider is finding the right school that will suit the child's learning style. Here are some suggestions about choosing a school for your child.

Know your child. Look deeper into his/her behavior; observe how he or she learns and how he or she is as a student. Does he or she learn better by touch or by listening? Is he or she the type that does well in a group or alone? Does he or she like to volunteer, or do you need to draw him/her out? You should also consider his/her specific needs, such as a seat far from the window (for fewer distractions) or a teacher who can give him/her step-by-step instructions.

Check out, possible candidates. Don't limit your research by just reading leaflets describing their services and academic accomplishments; get in-depth by interviewing teachers, guidance counselors, principals, and other special-needs providers. It is also essential to interview parents whose children are enrolled in the school to better view how the school works.

What Type of Students Will My Child Be Grouped with?

Of course, finding the right school is not the only thing you need to do to make sure your child is also getting the education he or she deserves. Cooperation with your child's teacher is also very important. Try to develop a better relationship with your child's teacher at the beginning of the school year. Set a meeting face-to-face with the teacher to talk about your child. Be honest about your expectations and worries, as well as provide tips that might be able to help the teacher handle your child when he or she becomes disruptive. It would also be a better idea to talk about what works with your child regarding his/her learning style. You can also set up regular contact with the teacher, such as weekly progress reports, daily phone calls, or emails.

It is also a good idea to ask about helpful classroom accommodations for your child, such as:

- A seating arrangement closer to the teaching area and farther away from possible distractions, such as a window or door.
- Reduced workload (both in homework and schoolwork) to take into account the child's attention span.

- Allowing extra time for the child to finish tests and assignments and providing a quiet space for him/ her to take these tests to avoid distractions.

Defiant Children & Nonverbal Communication

Why is it so important to understand the value of nonverbal communication in teaching and learning? In moments of high social pressure from peers, nonverbal communication will always be one of the most, if not the most, essential skills to possess. Social pressure brings about the times when humans will think the most thoughts in their heads, while also acting the least on those ideas. Where is social pressure always present? It is an educational atmosphere filled with teaching and learning. We'll discuss teaching and learning in the school setting primarily.

A teacher's inner dialogue commonly includes; what is the level of respect my students exhibit towards me? Are they listening and paying attention to my words? How can I be cool and relatable without crossing the line and becoming a pushover? Am I an effective teacher with helpful lessons? The list goes on forever.

Relating to Teachers

If you have a good working relationship with your instructor, you will encourage your child's progress at school. Yet partnerships can be compromised if you consider that his instructor is incompetent or if, conversely, his teacher thinks you are not doing an excellent parenting job. That can happen if there is no contact with you. So how do you develop a relationship with the teacher of your child?

Daily Reports

Term report cards for many years have been with us. Nevertheless, it is now customary to use daily reports to track children living with explosive synths. Regular updates have been widely accepted as they have some apparent advantages. Knowing what happened during your child's school day can be very helpful. Such data helps you to deal with problems efficiently and avoid them before they get worse.

Daily coverage can be troublesome as educators often pull parents into issues that can be easily handled throughout the day of class. As school issues leak into the evening hours, most parents are upset. Instead, such problems monopolize the family time, and parents are fearful of every report.

You can also be pushed into an official by the monitoring system. The child is likely to interpret school events in terms that put him in a favorable light, although his instructor is likely to point out that something entirely different has happened. Under these conditions, you might place a strain on your relationship with him if you criticize your child when you haven't seen what happened. On the other hand, if you are side by side with your child, you risk undermining his teacher's credibility. Sadly, if you take a stand against his instructor, you might encourage future non-cooperative activities. Your child may get the message that his teacher's conduct was inappropriate, and he may wonder if listening to her makes sense at all. In particular, if your child has often felt chastised at home, he might like the fact that you are now fighting for him instead of criticizing him. In class, he will continue to create drama because he loves your encouragement. As you can see, teacher upheaval poses the same kinds of issues as in family triangles.

Know the favorite activities of the rest of the students. If the whole classroom loves a certain privilege, then so will the defiant child due to the effect of herd behavior. No one enjoys being left out while they watch their peers have fun. If the child does not comply after the second command, you follow through with your threats, ignore them and focus on those who are doing great.

Nothing provides comfort to children like familiar surroundings, and their behavior is not as harshly judged by those who understand what they are going through.

When it comes to an explosive child, teachers, and parents are advised to use one of two strategies. These rules guide the dos and don'ts to make the child's school life easier.

In such an instance, if the teacher understood the child's needs and had provided the three questions instead, then the assignment would be submitted as complete, with enough effort placed in it. By avoiding long assignments, the child's first thought is not to just complete the assignment, so it is out of the way – but they put effort into it as well and in this way, they don't fail in class.

Consider a child who has difficulty organizing their work. They are constantly misplacing and forgetting their homework or which assignments must be completed first. It becomes chaotic and stressful for them, especially when the teacher is unsure how to assist.

The teacher may believe that things are not going well at home, which is stressing the child, and that calling the parent is not a good idea. They only have one other option, which is to assemble a person in a better position to study the child and advise on the best course of action to be taken. Then, once they are certain of what is going on, they involve the parent.

While parents often want to be the first to be notified, it should not bother them that the teacher sought outside help first because then this shows that they are just as invested in the child.

Punishments are learning experiences. They are not intended to cause the child pain, but rather to teach him or her. Punishing a child with disorder explosions with something that helps them gain control is not recommended. This would be physical exercise; punishing them by not allowing them to participate in sports, which would provide them with an outlet, would exacerbate their aggression and resentment.

Don't Use Negative Words

It is essential to insist on positivity while playing with a child with explosive attacks. It would work if you gave feedback but positively provide them so that your child's confidence level increases. If you keep making them feel that whatever they do is wrong, they will start feeling that no one loves them. That makes the outbursts worse and sometimes even out of control. The use of any form of harmful language is wrong for an explosive kid or all children.

Discipline for the Classroom

Defiant children enjoy pushing your buttons and finding out how much compliance they can get out of you! Yes, children naturally know how to get compliance out of adults. Heck, kids understand better than adults the best ways to achieve goals. Coming from infancy as babies who had to use nonverbal communication to get food, they depended on other people's willingness to comply with their requests. They used smiling, laughing, crying, pointing, and outright determination. On the other hand, adults become so prideful in their independence that they forget what it takes to get the most out of other people. It is important to understand when and how to discipline an oppositional defiant child. For example, a common defiant behavior is a child who tells authority figures "no" when it is time to put games away or complete classwork. You can simply ignore the child and give extra treats to those students who are listening. The defiant child wants you to beg them to complete their work. They want everyone in the class to look at them while you argue and try to sort out a solution. This is where a defiant child will try to embarrass your authority power. What is your resolution to this scenario? Give your command once (e.g., Get in line please). If they say no, try putting a consequence behind the command while still maintaining a calm voice (e.g., Get in line or you won't watch the movie later, get in line or go to the office). Here, you see that the consequence should be taking away a privilege that they love or one that involves the child having to deal with a higher authority figure (e.g. the principal or other high-power disciplinary figure in the school). Look the child directly in their eyes and ignore them if they fail to listen after the second time. It works in your favor and gains respect from the child because they know that you are not going to overreact to their defiance.

Strategies for Behavioral Disorder Treatment at School

Teachers frequently have a more difficult time dealing with children and cannot do it all on their own. As previously stated, when a parent drops their child off and calls it a day, they do not transfer responsibility to the teacher. There is much more at stake than simply attending PTA meetings at the school, and they must work together to help the child. There are, however, things both the parent and teacher can do to help the kid at school.

This responsibility doesn't always fall on just the two. The school, as an institution, also plays a role in this. They have a responsibility to educate their staff and other students about mental health issues. The school may decide to provide special education learning, not to separate the children by dividing them into different classes but to provide the children with an opportunity to learn and be among other people understand them.

Behavioral Management

This is just as the name suggests. Its focus is on the behavior of the child and how their emotions affect them. How teachers and parents handle a situation without undermining the child's self-esteem. Teachers understand how to help the child on a personal level, as well as the child's emotions and approach to situations. To avoid the development of negative behavior, this strategy entails encouraging positive behavior and rewarding it. All this without making the child feel like they are receiving preferential treatment.

Organization Management

One of the biggest challenges that explosive children

encounter in school is the ability to stay organized. Their explosions frequently produce sloppy work, and their lack of organization skills, as a result, disadvantages them in class performance. Helping the children with this goes a long way toward helping the child achieve better results, which in turn boosts their self-esteem.

Tips for Teachers

Provide Clear Assignment Instructions

When the teacher gives instructions, the child is frequently absent-minded and daydreaming, and he or she misses what is said. When the teacher realizes this about the child and that their behavior is not intentional, they devise strategies to ensure that the same information shared with the other children is not missed by the explosive child. How will they go about it? Questioning the student to see if they understand. They could also call the student after class and go over the assignment with them to ensure the student understands what is expected of them. In this case, it is also critical to check in on the student's assignment progress regularly.

Pay Attention to Behavior

Most teachers who work with teenagers and children are already familiar with and have experience with how children behave. They understand that passive aggression is very common in children and, as a result, they frequently ignore it. Teachers must become more aware of mental health issues and learn to recognize warning signs when behavior deviates from the norm. When a child is extremely agitated and continues to pick fights with everyone or speak back to the teacher to avoid being sent out of the classroom. Of course, is not an excuse for bad behavior, and such behavior should not be rewarded by not punishing it; however, there is a source for that behavior, and punishing the child without addressing the source of the problem does not accomplish much.

Sensitize Themselves on Explosive Disorder Influence on Emotions

Teachers' reactions to explosive students can make or break them. Children who are unable to focus long enough to complete their tasks are sensitive to criticism. At this point, the children believe what adults in positions of authority tell them. It is very easy to break a child's spirit by verbally attacking them when they are unable to complete a project instead of helping them get past it.

Teachers must understand why those children behave the way they do. Always engaging in risky activities, he is sometimes referred to as the "class clown" by his peers.

Avoid Long and Repetitive Assignments

This is related to the attention span issue. Long

assignments easily bore and distract explosive children. Returning to the previous example of a child skipping five questions because they know that if they put effort into the work, they will only manage three and mark the assignment as incomplete. However, if you just do all five with no effort, the assignment is complete, even if it is done poorly.

Allow Breaks

Teachers need to encourage movement and exercise. A one-and-a-half-hour class is taxing on any child, not just those with the disorder. Half an hour has passed, and the child is already bored out of their minds, their attention diverted elsewhere. A teacher can come up with a way to make the class more interesting by involving the students. Keep them talking. Incorporate stories into the lesson, or even have them stand for a few minutes. Explosive children have a very short attention span and find it difficult to concentrate, so making classwork something they enjoy and look forward to can help.

Apply Organization Tools

This has proven to be a very effective method. This includes the use of tools like files, folders, and lists. This is meant to help children keep track of the things they need to do and trace their activities. An explosive child already struggles with organizational skills and is easily distracted. Keeping a file with their homework allows the child and parent to track progress and serves as a reminder for the child when they forget to do something. They can always return to the folder or list to see what is expected of them.

Minimize Distractions

Children can be easily distracted by the smallest things. During class, the teacher should discourage interruptions to ensure the children focus on the lesson. Teachers would always aim to have their students learn something at the end of the day. This is impossible to achieve if there are constant distractions. While children who do not have any disorder can recover from a distraction and return their attention to their teacher, those who do have explosive disorder find it difficult to concentrate once the focus has been lost.

Communicate with Parents

Communication between the parent and the teacher should be the first step to take before making further decisions, such as involving a counselor. The first thing that a teacher should do when they notice that a child's behavior is not typical is to contact the parent. The parents understand their child best—the teacher can have conversations with them, and exchange notes to see if the child's behavior is exclusive to school grounds or if it happens everywhere.

Involve School Guidance and Counselor

In most cases, this follows after contacting the parent. However, a teacher may be suspicious of a child's behavior but be unsure whether their suspicions are correct or not. Guidance counselors at school are more than just teachers. Teachers are not expected to know everything, so having someone point out things they do not understand helps.

Create Clear Rules

Teachers need to create rules and state the consequences when children fail to follow them. As stated earlier, while explosive disorder is a mental disorder that limits a child's executive functions, children with this condition are still children. The condition should not be used to excuse bad behavior. When they break the rules, they should receive punishment for their actions and reward when they do good.

Try to Make Learning Fun

Very few children enjoy learning, and they will all give you different reasons why it is not fun for them. Engaging children in studies has proven to be a beneficial method, and the children who require this type of learning the most are those with explosive disorders.

Those children respond better to things that interest them—when an assignment is made to be a game, they will want to play. This is like what parents do at home to make sure their child is engaged in the work they are doing. Using apples to help with their math problems, using other fruits to help with identifying color, or silly acronyms, and letting the creative side of the child influence their studies.

CHAPTER 14

How to Best Manage Home Study and Time and Keep Their Attention High

As parents, we have to do what we can to deal with the school workload and help our children do their homework faithfully and to a high quality. That takes time and perseverance, but it is worth it. How can we, as parents, encourage our children to do their homework?

There is nothing worse than spending your afternoon or evening battling with your child or teen about homework. You may feel like a nag, he or she may feel like you're overbearing, and it's hard on the relationship. The ultimate goal is to make homework time a more pleasant experience for everyone involved. The first step is to evaluate why it's a battle in the first place. Is homework too easy? Too hard? Too long? Not stimulating? Overwhelming? Okay, for some subjects or tasks but not for others? The intervention will vary depending on the reason homework is a struggle for your child. Ask your child's teacher if he or she observes resistance to specific subjects or tasks. Inquire about your child's skill level in each subject and ensure that failure to complete tasks is not due to a lack of understanding.

It is also essential to discuss with your child the rationale behind homework. Homework serves to strengthen or extend the skills learned at school, teaches responsibility, and perhaps most importantly, gives the teacher feedback about what concepts are reliable and what else needs to be taught. When you frame homework as information for the teacher, your child may be more responsive and less defensive than if you present it as a necessary evil in their life.

Sometimes kids who seek plenty of attention from you during homework time may be seeking connection. Instead of thinking he or she should just be independent, think about homework time as a way to connect to your child. Learn what he or she is learning about, and you can have exciting discussions together. Work through difficult tasks together, and your child will view you as a supportive person in his/her life. Some parents will choose the work they have to do and sit with their child while he or she does homework. That can send an implicit message that everyone has work to do, and it can be more pleasurable when you have a work companion.

Cooperate with the School

Knowing that our child may have an explosive disorder problem, we must work with the school about expectations within the classroom and the school. If there need to be extensions on homework assignments, we need to communicate with teachers. They need to be aware of the situation so they can help. Asking your school to provide accommodation for your child is essential, so you should request that your school cooperate with you to support what he needs to succeed at school.

Help Your Child Get Started and Help Them If They Don't Understand Anything

Always be encouraging your child to do their homework. Tell them that they are working as if school is their job and needs to do good work to receive remuneration. Help your child realize the importance of responsibility and doing things the right way. Also, teach your child about how vital it is to do their homework, not only for getting a good grade but for facilitating the learning process and growing and developing as a person.

Teach Your Child How to Do Their Homework Mindfully

Then, teach your child some skills that will help them to do their homework mindfully. Homework can be stressful for some kids, especially young ones, but you can bring mindful awareness to your body and mind before doing the homework or taking a test. Here are steps your child can take to do their homework mindfully.

1. Sit comfortably in a chair. Find a resting position to be upright and relax.
2. Place your hands down in your lap or on the table in front of you
3. Sit in silence, open your ears, and concentrate on the sounds coming from the room next to you.
4. Put your hand(s) on your stomach. And notice how your stomach is moving up and down with each breath. Take in four to five deep breaths.
5. Be mindful of how your body feels and if you feel anxious, continue deep breathing exercises.
6. Now, you're able to complete all your assignments with the right amount of ease and perseverance.
7. At the end of homework time, you can say to your

child, "good job! You did great!" You can be friendly and kind to a child by congratulating their hard work and effort.

Encourage and Compliment Your Child

As your child is doing his or her homework, you must provide them with a lot of praise and encouragement. When you see that they are focusing and concentrating for longer than thirty minutes, tell them: "you're doing a great job. I see you have been working hard. Keep doing it!" Children especially need to receive a fair amount of praise to get them going and keep them doing what they want them to do. In particular, the young ones need a lot of it, because they are quite sensitive and prone to emotional challenges. And, say all of your praises and encouragement with genuineness and integrity. You must mean everything that you speak to them so that it's not like you're just buttering them up.

Take Breaks

Just as it is essential to give your child a lot of encouragement, it is also necessary for you to schedule mental and physical breaks to do the homework. Your child, who has the explosive disorder, will likely be unable to concentrate for longer than 15 minutes at a time. Their mind will wander and be at a different place within 10 minutes, so you must provide them with the time and space to go outside and get a refresher from Mother

Nature. It is also essential that your child not spend too much at a desk in a stationary position. It is not suitable for their back or overall health. Don't let your child work too hard without giving them a well-deserved break. Please give them a glass of ice-cold milk or an apple to provide them with an energy boost to keep going with the work.

Establish a Rewards System to Encourage Your Child

Along with scheduling mental breaks from homework, it is essential that you also provide them with a rewards system. You should be generous in giving your child rewards for a job well done, an "A" on a test, or a diligent attitude toward studying.

Establishing what is considered positive behavior is very important. It can be a good thing to help increase a child's self-esteem. It can also be a very good thing to make a home where good behavior is natural, fun, and expected. It is very important to back up rewards in a way that your child knows that you mean what you say.

CHAPTER 15
Healthy Diet Priority: Foods to Eat, Foods to Avoid

They are the foods and supplements you take. Your daily diet plans should help your brain function well and reduce symptoms, such as restlessness or inability to sustain concentration.

You could focus on these choices:

- **Overall nutrition.** The assumption is that the foods you eat will make your symptoms better or worse. You might not be eating some foods that might help you get better.
- **Supplements.** With this, you add nutritional supplements, nutrients, and vitamins to your diet. The theory is that it could help you make up for the inadequate nutrient. It is believed that if you don't get enough nourishment, it could worsen your symptoms
- **Remove diets.** This involves not eating foods or things that trigger your symptoms or worsen them.

Top Foods for the Explosive Disorder

- **Additive-free and unprocessed foods.** Due to the harmful nature of additives, you should eat fresh and unprocessed foods. Additives include artificial sweeteners, preservatives, and colorings which can be found in processed foods, they are detrimental to explosive children.
- **Chicken.** Tryptophan is an essential amino acid

that helps the body synthesize proteins and help with the creation of serotonin. Serotonin induces sleep, happy emotions, and helps with impulse control and hostility.

- **Eat breakfast.** For most children with explosive disorders, breakfast helps the body regulate bloodstream sugars and stabilize hormonal fluctuations. Eat breakfast that has at least 20 grams of proteins. Try my Thin Mint Proteins Smoothie which has 20 grams of proteins; it is a delicious and filling way to "break the fast."
- **Wild-caught salmon.** It is not only rich in vitamin B-6 but is also filled with omega 3. According to the institution of Maryland hospital, a scientific trial indicated that lower examples of omega-3 EFA's solved learning and behavioral problems (like those related to disorder explosions) than kids with reasonable levels of omega. Individuals, including children, should eat healthy salmons at least twice a week.

Foods to Avoid

- **Sugar.** This is the main trigger for children. Avoid any type of refined sugar including chocolate, desserts, soda, or fruit drinks.
- **Gluten.** Some researchers and parents observe worsening behavior when a child eats gluten, which can indicate sensitivity to the protein in wheat. Avoid all foods made with whole wheat grains such as bread, pasta, and whole wheat

grains cereal. Seek out gluten-free and even grain-free alternatives.

- **Milk products.** Most cow milk contains A1 that may trigger the same reaction as gluten and, so should be avoided. If severe symptoms occur after eating milk products, discontinue use. Goat's milk doesn't include proteins and it is a better option for explosive children.
- **Food color and dyes.** Children could be allergic to food dyes and colorings; therefore, all processed foods should be avoided. Colorings and dyes can be found in nearly every commercially prepared food. Food dyes can be found in energy drinks, chocolates, wedding cakes mix, chewable nutritional supplements as well as toothpaste!
- **Caffeine.** Even though some studies prove that caffeine might help with some behavioral disorder symptoms, it pays to lessen or avoid caffeine, however, even these studies haven't been validated. The side-effect of caffeine, include anxiousness, and nervousness. All these can further worsen the explosive symptoms.
- **MSG and HVP.** These additives are believed to lessen dopamine amounts in children and adults. Dopamine is from the brain's pleasure and prize systems. For children battling with behavioral disorder explosions, well-balanced dopamine is essential.
- **Nitrites.** Commonly found in lunch meat, canned foods, and several processed foods. Nitrites are connected with a child's growth, type one

diabetes, certain types of malignancy, and IBS. It could result in an increased heartbeat, difficulty breathing, and restlessness that aggravate explosive disorder explosions symptoms.

- **Artificial sweeteners.** Artificial sweeteners are harmful to your health, and for dealing with the behavioral disorder; the unwanted effects could be damaging. Artificial sweeteners create biochemical adjustments in the body, which can affect cognitive function and psychological balance.

- **Allergens/Things that trigger allergies.** Eliminate the top seven allergens, including soy, wheat, and milk, peanuts, tree nuts, eggs, and shellfish. Furthermore, eliminate any foods or drinks that are personal contaminants in the air. This may include papaya, avocados, bananas, kiwis (for people with latex allergies), coriander, caraway or fennel (all the same family), and chocolates.

Supplements for the Explosive Disorder

Some experts advise that explosive children take 100% vitamin and nutrient supplements each day. Other diet experts believe that individuals who take balanced meals don't need a supplement or micronutrient supplements. They claim there is no scientific evidence that vitamin or mineral supplements help all those with the disorder. While multivitamins would help for children, teens, and adults who don't balance their meals, several doses of vitamins could be toxic, avoid them.

Symptoms of explosive disorder differ from person to person. Work closely with a medical doctor, if you're taking supplements. To help yourself, you need to identify the food that is making your symptoms worse and endeavor to eliminate it from your diet. If the symptoms disappear, ensure you steer clear of the food and avoid it entirely.

If you cut out your favorite food from your daily diet, does your symptom worsen? Research is ongoing in this area, and the details aren't explicit.

Iron Supplementation

More studies are being conducted that show the effects low iron can have on children. When we think of a lack of iron, we think of those that are suffering from blood loss. When our bodies are lacking this basic mineral, a lot can happen, including an increase in our disorder explosions symptoms. It affects more than you might expect.

Iron is important to our bodies because it is what is responsible for making sure that oxygen makes its way to our vital organs and all of our muscles. We also need it for proper brain function. When we are lacking iron, it can also slow the production of dopamine, which is essential for those that want to live a happy, healthy life. If our explosive symptoms are out of control, then it might be a sign that we need more iron in our lives and diets.

Omega 3/6

By this point, you should have a basic understanding of just how important dopamine is for proper brain function. Recent studies have shown that increasing the amount of good fat we eat, including in omega-rich foods, can help regulate the normal production of dopamine in our brains.

These fatty acids will improve brain function. While doing this, they will also increase attention. When brain function and attention increase, disorder explosions symptoms dramatically decrease. Along with more attention, these supplements can also help lessen restlessness, impulsivity, hyperactivity, and overall aggression in children. Some scientists even believe this is the best treatment for those that don't want to use any other medications.

Most researchers don't recommend this technique for controlling explosive disorder, however here are some common concerns and what professionals suggest: Food additives: In 1975, an allergist initially proposed that artificial colors, flavors, and preservatives might trigger hyperactivity in a few children. Child behavior experts have extensively argued this matter. Some said the thought of eliminating these ingredients from the diet is unfounded and unsupported by technology. However, one research demonstrates that food color and preservatives do increase hyperactivity in some children. However, the effects vary with age and type of additive.

Sugars: Some children become hyperactive after eating chocolate or other sugary foods. No study has proven that this triggers disorder explosions, however, sugary foods are best avoided.

Children that were given fish oil supplements were found to be better at reading and spelling, with overall improvements in their behavior as well. This means that kids can benefit greatly from including this supplement in their diet. In addition, it is one of the top natural depression fighters out there. As adults, we get even more health benefits from improving our omega-3 and 6 fatty acid consumption beyond just the reduction of our disorder explosions symptoms. These include an increase in eye health and a lower risk of heart disease developing.

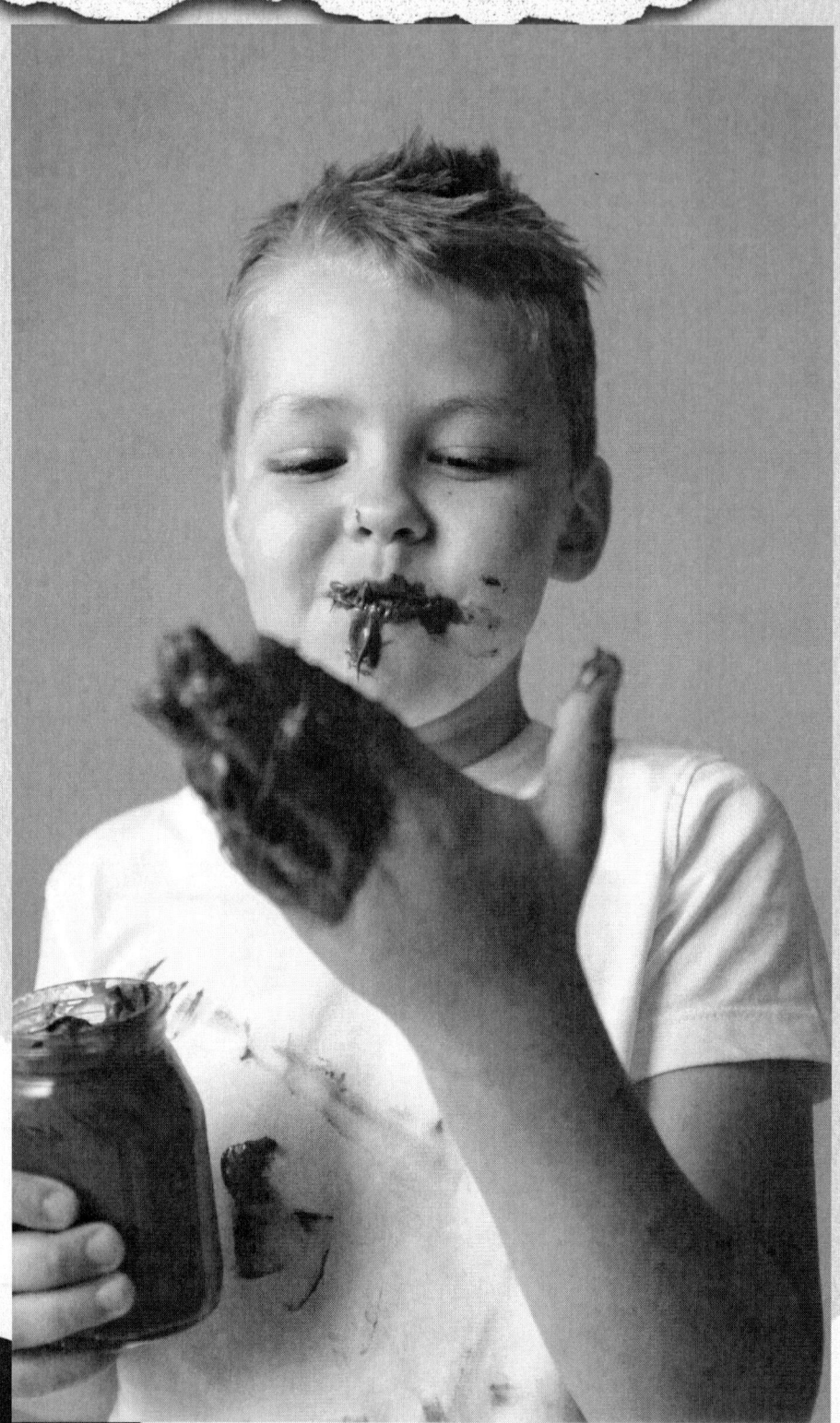

CHAPTER 16
7 Strategies to Disciplining Explosive Kids

The fact that children who are reared with clear limits and direction are more likely to be happy, pleasant people with good self-control is one of the many essential reasons why you should discipline your children.

Children who have been indulged and who have been given no limits or penalties are generally greedy, unable to self-regulate, and unpleasant to be around.

The solution: Set clear and consistent rules, boundaries, and consequences for your child when he or she does not follow them. Keep the broader picture in mind if you're scared that disciplining your child may make them upset. A child's future will suffer if they are not disciplined. As long as you're in charge of them, give them good penalties with love and respect.

Positive Discipline

Positive discipline is worth a try if you've never felt comfortable spanking your child. Without resorting to threats, incentives, scolding, or physical punishment, you can often nip undesirable behavior in the bud by utilizing positive disciplinary strategies like redirection, praise, and selective ignoring. This disciplining strategy, according to proponents, can help develop ties and increase trust between parents and children. When you respond to provocation with these five tried-and-true examples of constructive discipline instead of anger, you're also teaching a youngster that it's possible to deal with difficult situations without getting into a fight.

Redirection

Little ones have a short attention span, so redirecting them to another activity when they're acting out isn't difficult. Introduce another item that will capture your toddler's attention if he or she is playing with a potentially unsafe object. If that doesn't work, take them to a different room or outside to distract them.

Instead of telling an older youngster what they can't do, tell them what they can. Rather than telling your youngster that they can no longer watch YouTube, tell them that they may go outdoors and play or work on a new puzzle. Focusing on the good can help you avoid a lot of fights and stubborn behavior.

An exceptional method for diffusing defiance and conflict rapidly is called redirection. When you redirect your child's focus, you are essentially breaking their attention away from one thing and guiding it toward something more positive. Turning their attention away from a trigger and toward a solution is an excellent example of redirection, though it can be achieved in many other ways, too.

If your child tends to habitually respond to certain triggers overwhelmingly, now is an excellent opportunity to practice redirecting their attention before the explosive outburst toward a peaceful outcome. Learning to correctly perform this particular redirect will affect your child's habitual response into a more productive process, effectively diffusing any conflict before it arises.

For example, let's say putting your child's shoes on so you can leave the house is a common point of conflict, and every time you ask them to put their shoes on they are triggered. You may notice that you tend to state the need to put their shoes on as follows: "Can you please put your shoes on so we can go grocery shopping?" At this point, you have already lost your child's attention at the point of asking them to put their shoes on, and they have begun melting down before you even finished your sentence. Instead, you might say, "We need to go buy some more of your favorite snacks so you can have them to eat for school! Put your shoes on so we can go. [Hand them their shoes.] What flavor will you pick this time?" Following the second example, you emphasize focusing on the benefit they are getting from going out and minimizing the stress of putting their shoes on. As long as you keep them distracted and sell them on the benefits of going out, it is likely that they will put their shoes on quickly so they can enjoy the aforementioned benefits.

You can perform this sort of redirection in absolutely any situation you find yourself in with your child, regardless of the subject of that situation. For it to be productive, though, you need to know what your child does not want to do, and what they do want to do. Structure your delivery by selling them on the benefit of getting to do what they want to do before asking them about what they tend to be triggered by. In turn, you maintain their positive attention, and they are more likely to comply.

Discourage Yelling in the Home

While yelling across the house may seem like an easier way to get your child's attention than, say, walking over to their room and talking to them, this can foster an increasingly stressful environment. Yelling through the door or wall at your child, or allowing them to yell at you this way, can set the tone for meltdowns rather quickly. During the yelling process, everyone is already elevating their energy through the simple act of shouting. Further, miscommunications are far more likely under these circumstances, and that can make for even larger meltdowns if you are not careful.

Rather than welcoming screaming as a means of communication, set a rule that everyone must speak within close enough proximity that you can converse with a calm voice. This means no more yelling across the house or through walls to communicate. Instead, you can either walk to each other and start talking or knock on a bedroom door and wait to be invited in before you start talking to each other. This way, yelling is discouraged, and peaceful, respectful communication is encouraged instead.

Connection before Correction

Taking the time to connect with your child by hugging them and affirming that you love them before you begin correcting their behavior ensures that they receive the support they require to navigate their troubling emotions, first. You can then discuss what was wrong with their behavior and educate them on a more positive means for dealing with their emotions in the future.

Set Limits in a Loving Way

Punishment is typically used as a means of setting limits, though it is often allotted negatively or critically. Learning to set limits affectionately allows you to acknowledge and correct negative behavior without exploding into rages of anger or otherwise experiencing an undesirably emotional outburst with your child. For instance, let's imagine that your child wants to keep playing their game instead of getting ready for bed, so they start having a meltdown or show the early stages of an emotional outburst due to their desire to keep playing. Rather than retorting with "Too bad" or "It's time for bed, so stop playing, NOW!" you might try something along the lines of: "Wow you're enjoying this game aren't you! I understand it's hard to stop playing and get ready for bed. Let's continue with this game tomorrow." This way, you are acknowledging your child's feelings, having empathy for them, and still upholding the limits so you can encourage your child to do as they have been asked.

Teach Your Kid to Fix Their Mistakes

Making mistakes is an inevitable part of life, but children may be more prone to them, considering they have not learned from many of their own mistakes in the past. Further, they have not had the opportunity to properly learn how to adapt and navigate their mistakes, either. Teaching your child how to address and remedy their mistakes ensures they recognize how to overcome any potential adversities, and in turn, are more likely to navigate them peacefully.

When it comes to teaching your child how to navigate mistakes, always do so in a matter-of-fact way. Do not make a big deal about the mistake, as doing so can trigger a huge emotional response, and that can make dealing with the mistake far more challenging. Instead, acknowledge that a mistake happened and focus on fixing the mistake with your child, so they realize mistakes are not worth a major emotional outcry, and that they can easily be resolved and worked out.

Time-In

Time-out can be an effective punishment, but it can be difficult to execute properly. According to research, 85 percent of parents who try to use this disciplinary technique backfire, such as talking with kids or letting them play with toys during time-outs. (Time-outs should be solitary and boring to be most effective.) If your instinct is to interact with your child rather than banish them, you might try a time-in. Rather than putting your child to time-out alone after a period of bad conduct, sit down with them and read a book together.

Time-ins are useful in and of themselves for promoting good conduct, but they are most successful when combined with well-executed time-outs regularly.

CHAPTER 17
DISCIPLINE VS. CONSEQUENCE VS. PUNISHMENT

Discipline techniques for other children might not work for explosive children, but there must be boundaries and codes of conduct established. That kid needs a firm but loving hand when being corrected. You must fight to control your anger even when the child displays unacceptable behavior or is refusing to follow instructions. Removing privileges such as time playing computer games or looking at television is one way of dispensing discipline. Time outs are also a favorite for parents of those children. They should be put into effect as soon as the infringement is committed and should not last too long because the child won't complete it, and the effect will be lost. You also have to be careful not to transfer your frustration at your child to your other children as they could end up being scolded a lot more severely than they deserved to be simply because you needed an outlet for your anger.

A sense of humor is precious in a home with an explosive child. You should learn to laugh instead of being embarrassed every time your child does things that might be socially unacceptable in a public place. It won't be easy but try to remember that the embarrassment will pass in time, and all that will be left would be a fun story to relate to your friends and relatives. Sometimes it is okay to ignore the bad behavior once it is not causing anyone, including the child himself, any harm. That is not suggested as an ongoing way of dealing with tantrums and other misbehavior forms, but sometimes it is the right material to do. Those children need constant attention, and to get it, they would be willing to misbehave because negative attention is still attention. If your child is complaining and arguing for no reason, ignore him/her until it stops. If the complaining accelerates, let the child know that you would not be responding until he or she clams down. Like everything else, this will be successful sometimes but won't work in every instance. You will have to gauge when it is the right time to use it.

Your child is going to make many mistakes. Learn to compromise by letting the small ones pass. Pick your battles carefully and deal with issues individually. Don't try to solve every problem at once because that is setting yourself up for disappointment. Through all the challenges, never stop believing in your child and his/her ability to overcome. Make this clear to the child as well; he or she should know at all times that you believe in them. Stay positive. Encourage your child to vocalize their feelings. If he or she can tell you when he or she is feeling sad or angry, you might help them understand the problem before it leads to an episode of bad behavior.

Children with explosive disorder have to adhere to the family's rules and home they live in just as other children do because they are usually disorganized and impulsive, they need a structured existence even more than others. Make the rules very clear to the child so they know precisely what is expected of them. Break down instructions into simple steps and speak in the most precise and most straightforward of ways. Look straight with your child's eyes when speaking to him/

her to know that he or she is attracted to you and what you are saying. Make him/her repeat what you said back to you, so you know that he or she has heard it. Many parents have found it helpful to engage in role-playing with their child to link him/her between his/her behavior and the reaction of his/her parent to it. Those children can often make that connection and establish it to help minimize unacceptable behavior.

These rules may need explaining a bit more often than with other children, so you have to be patient but persistent and keep repeating the limits until they get it. Make the child understand that if the rules aren't followed, there will be consequences such as no television or spending time in his/her room, and if need be, those consequences will be implemented.

Positive and Negative Discipline Are Two Different Types of Discipline

Positive discipline inspires children to make better choices by guiding them toward more productive activities and praising them when they behave well, whereas negative discipline tends to involve sanctions and admonishing words in an attempt to prevent them from acting badly.

With highly negative behaviors we must resort to punishment, to mitigate or decrease them. Punishment should never be used alone, it goes along with the positive increase techniques described above. The use of punishment is reinforcing for the adult: it makes him feel "the strongest," the "outburst" vents, immediately relieves tension... Its educational use, however, is more controversial than it may appear!

How to Positively Discipline a Child

Before you lose your cool when your child misbehaves, realize that it is not their fault, nor yours. Discipline must be approached differently for explosive children.

Disciplining your children is unlikely to be among your top-five favorite aspects of parenting but keep in mind that you're not on your own. There's a lot of study on techniques you can use to make discipline simpler for you and your kids. Read on to learn what works, what doesn't, and how to care for your nerves when they're stressed.

Parental Discipline Begins with Their Discipline

Children invariably respond to the parent's behavior. So be conscious of your stress levels and how they may affect your child. A good recommendation is for parents to conduct relaxation and deep breathing exercises for at least 10 seconds before talking to their kids when stressed out.

Routine and Consistency Help to Prevent Outbursts Before They Occur

Routine and structure are incredibly crucial for children with disorder explosions. Here is how you can put it into action:

- **Have regular schedules for school, homework, extracurricular activities, time with friends, and bedtimes.** All are essential in helping children in remaining energetically and emotionally regulated to avoid at least some aggression from occurring.
- **A well-balanced meal plan.** Disorder explosions symptoms can be managed effectively with continuous exercise and a good meal-plan
- **Get enough rest.** Researchers discovered that low sleep quality and daytime sleepiness were linked to impaired executive functioning in children with disorder explosions.

Children's Timeouts Must Be Planned and Specified

To avoid confusion, you should make it obvious which actions are on the list. And when such behaviors occur, you can do the following:

Recognize and Reward Positive Behavior While Ignoring Unpleasant Outbursts

Kids are subjected to a lot of criticism, and over time, they come to anticipate it. So rather than focusing on unpleasant outbursts, focusing on their positive behaviors will make your life and that of your child easier.

According to some researchers, given that every child reacts to things differently, rewarding positive actions might have the opposite impact, undermining child-rearing for some children and teenagers.

This is why it's important to pay attention to your child's response and take an unbiased look to see if they're learning the character behind the positive behavior or just doing what they have to do to get the reward.

Reward Only Those Who Deserve It

It's critical to be specific in your praise if you're going to employ a reward system. You don't have to claim your child did an "excellent job" just because they cleaned their room or didn't engage in undesirable conduct.

Instead, compliment them on the level of work they put into tidying their room. Also, avoid praising insignificant achievements or half-hearted attempts.

Children with an explosive disorder do have problems managing their behavior when rewards were inconsistent or the relationship between actions (their behavior) and a result (possible rewards) is unclear. To maximize the chances of getting the best results from them, parents should be consistent and clear in their rewards.

What to Say and Must Never Say to Your Child

You may be at a loss for words if your child has recently been diagnosed with disorder explosions. Here's how you can communicate the situation to them, while also building them up.

Do's and Don'ts When Discussing Explosive Disorder with Your Child

- **Maintain an optimistic attitude:** When speaking with your child, this is the most vital thing to consider. If youngsters can see their disorder as a tool or something they can creatively utilize in the world rather than a barrier or problem to overcome, there are numerous potentials for personal growth.

  You will have to embrace a growth mentality when dealing with your kid. If a child can't accomplish something, it's because they can't do it yet; they can improve and work on it later.

  With time, commitment and experience, instructors and parents can help their kids organize their external environment by making it part of the child's education, so they can learn to handle it on their own.

- **Prepare them for success:** Disorder explosions do not imply that your child is incapable of focusing or completing tasks. If they are interested in anything, they can focus on it strongly, to the point that it is difficult to redirect their attention. You can assist them in focusing by learning about their passions and creating a series of simple tasks that will demonstrate to them how well they can pay attention if they use their disorder explosions constructively.

What you could say: "disorder explosions don't define who you are," "There are many gifted people with disorder explosions. It just means you learn things uniquely and differently," "There is nothing wrong with them. Your brain just functions differently from that of others in that it works a bit faster and slowing it down can be difficult at times. But that's why, during class, we practice sitting still."

Don'ts When Discussing disorder explosions with Your Child

- **Do not chastise them:** Remember that even if your child appears to be deliberately pushing your buttons, they haven't been given the tools to handle their specific kind of disorder explosions. Your child isn't trying to irritate you on purpose all of the time.

  If your child's hyperactivity is pushing them to run about the house all the time, keep in mind that they aren't acting out of a want to be disruptive; rather, they are acting out of an impulse desire to move their body.

  They'll start to better manage their urges and

outbursts as they learn to grasp their disorder explosions and find better ways to control themselves (such as through a behavioral management plan).

It's also not a good idea to use a recent incident to start the conversation regarding their behavioral disorder. Because your emotions are likely to be heightened, it's preferable to have the conversation in a quiet, distraction-free environment.

- **Don't make them feel bad about having disorder explosions:** It is a regular observation from most parents and teachers to frequently tell explosive kids that they are bad or dysfunctional. Spend less time focusing on what they're doing wrong and more time equipping them with knowledge of how unique and good they are.

Things to stay away from saying: "You're a child with a mental issue. That's just who you are," "Your life will be difficult, messy, and disorganized because of your problem," "You'll always struggle with learning things."

The Cost of Response

Usually, gratifications are effective, but sometimes it is necessary to think of a "point" system, like stars or smiles... that allows for immediate gratification, but of course symbolic, that can then be converted into other types of "rewards":

1. Define with the child the correct behaviors that will be rewarded.
2. Allocate points in proportion to the "effort" for the child (e.g., throwing the papers in the trash 1 point, doing all the homework 5 points).
3. Make a list with the child of things that are pleasant for him (e.g., a recess bonus, an assignment, a toy, a discount on an undesirable task…), find the correspondence with the number of points.
4. Determine what causes you to lose points and how many points you lose (this is the cost of the answer).
5. Always respect the agreements for the exchange.

It may be helpful to make a chart sign, so progress is perceptible to the child and, why not, to the rest of the class.

Always accompany the administration of points with social rewards.

If we anticipate a "fine" in the form of an unwanted deprivation or activity, we must administer it without anger, directly and simply, and without further delay or explanation. Example: "You pulled Mary's hair causing her to cry, you will lose ten minutes of break time by sitting in class alone. I don't want to hear any protests." Discussion closed.

Make the Most of a Time-Out

Time outs can be very effective if done correctly. They must be placed in an isolated place away from all distractions and interactions with other children. This can be very unpleasant for a disorder explosions child that craves distractions and stimulation. Make sure you give a clear command and set a time limit for them to comply. Make eye contact and use a firm tone of voice without yelling the instructions at them. Let them know in no uncertain terms why they are being taken to time-out and leave them there for the allotted time. Wait until the child is quiet and then repeat your command. If the child still does not wish to comply, then send them back to time-out. If they agreed or promise not to repeat the bad behavior, you can praise them for following your instructions.

If the child tries to escape, firmly put them back in the chair and repeat the instructions. If they persist, then you can give them a fine if you're using the point system or you can send them to another location void of all distractions. Make sure it is a place they cannot escape from.

When faced with a sudden behavior (an explosion of anger, destructiveness, something uncontrollable...) that we cannot prevent, it is useful to provide a timeout (see basket): remove the child from the situation in which the behavior occurred to prevent it from continuing. This is useful for impulsive and violent behaviors, certainly not for behaviors like not doing homework or not being able to sit still!

By suspending the child from the situation, you deprive him of attention or stimulation, you put him in an environment without attractions, where he has no opportunity to do anything. It is, therefore, necessary to first identify an environment with these characteristics, with a timeout corner (e.g. a corner of the classroom or a room where the child can sit still for a while, calculating a stillness of one minute for each year of age of the child). It is not correct to use the timeout as a threat (if you don't stop throwing toys, I'll...) but just do it, then invite the child to reflect. If the behavior is repeated: "you have thrown toys again, now you are going to be isolated for a while to think".

Your child must remember that "no" means "no" the first time. This can be regarding playtime, cleaning up, going to school, or anything else in their life. If they whine about it, you can give them a warning. This will be their chance to improve their behavior. If they continue to whine, you can implement a punishment. This is how you will get your child to learn that whining is not going to get them what they want: It will end up getting them the exact opposite.

Maximize Positive Attention for Your Child

Neurodivergent children often receive a great deal of negative attention from the world around them. For many of these children, something as simple as having a negative reaction to their surroundings can leave them questioning themselves and the world around them. Having a life constantly filled with overwhelming events, punishment, and a negative stigma from society can be extremely exhausting. Further, it feels like no one is rooting for them, so your child does not feel overly compelled to listen to anyone or please anyone.

Avoid Power Struggles

Children with behavioral disorders may engage in lengthy and exhausting power struggles with their parents, to get their way. Power struggles are signs of a child wanting to be in control of their own life and expecting everything to go their way regardless of what is right or wrong. In some cases, such as with children who have disorder explosions, they may be particularly wise at luring you into lengthy debates that end in a power struggle. As the parent, you must avoid these power struggles because regardless of how they seem, they are not productive or helpful to your situation in any shape or form.

Anytime you ask your child to complete a task, and they combat your direction, refrain from engaging back and forth in a debate. The longer you are arguing with your child, the longer it takes them to clean their room, brush their teeth or get ready for an outing. Instead of arguing, provide your child with clear instructions and clear consequences they will have to face if they do not clean their room, and if your commands are not fulfilled, follow through on those consequences.

Never attempt to force your child to complete a task. Nagging, arguing, or yelling at your child will remain entirely ineffective. Instead, set clear boundaries that make it unpleasant for them to ignore your requests and let them know after one warning that if they do not listen, they will face those unpleasant consequences. Always follow through, your child must respect your word and your authority. Otherwise, your bluff will be called, and the acts of defiance will develop considerably worse as your child learns to outmaneuver your leniency.

Create Clear, Easy to Follow Rules

Those children may struggle with rules because they do not comprehend, seemingly forget, or lack awareness of them entirely. Children with behavioral disorders like ODD or ADHD know what the rules are but will often willingly defy them or argue about them, looking for a way to push their buttons and break the rules altogether to suit their agenda.

A great way to reduce disagreements and minimize meltdowns is to establish clear household rules and regularly remind your child of them. Again, refrain from engaging in power struggles around these rules by refusing to argue about them, instead of having clear-cut consequences of what will happen if your child fails to respect those rules. It can be highly effective to post the household rules in a prominent area of your house, such as on your fridge, so your child can see them each day. If required, refer to the list of rules to remind your child of what the household guidelines are, as this prevents them from arguing with you and helps them behave by giving them something clear and focused to reflect on.

Have a Plan for Addressing Their Behavior

Instead of trying to fit them into a cookie-cutter approach, focus on creating a behavioral plan that specifically meets the needs of your child. An excellent way to create a robust and well-rounded plan that is reasonable for your child to follow is by creating one with their doctor and therapists. This way, your child's doctor and therapists can also discuss the strategy and information relating to it, hopefully helping your child get on the right track and follow your requests more easily.

When a behavioral plan has been prepared, it should include consequences that they will receive when they break the rules, and these consequences should be clearly explained ahead of time so that your child is well aware of what to expect. Often, these clear expectations avoid many meltdowns because your child already knows what to expect; therefore, they are less likely to try and push your boundaries. However, they may still try the first few times until they discover that you are not budging on your decision to enforce the promised consequences. Once they know you mean what you say, they will become far more likely to listen.

Use the Word "Yes" More Often

A great way to encourage your child to follow your guidance is to use the word "yes" more often. The more you can say yes, the more likely your child will be to listen because they feel a positive association with the word itself.

For example, if you exclaim "No, you cannot keep playing because you need to go to bed," or "No you cannot do that you need to get dressed," you are advocating the word "no" a lot. Your child perpetually hears every "no" and grows increasingly frustrated with each one, initiating a decline in receptivity toward you. Instead, you could insist; "Yes, it is time for bed, I'd love for you to show me your game tomorrow?" Or "Yes, you can do that after you get dressed." Or "Yes, I love you, and I am so lucky to be your parent. YES!" This type of affirmative response encourages positive emotions within your child, which inspires a far more likely inclination to listen and do what you have asked them to do.

Build Your Relationship Daily

Part of creating the opportunity for your child to listen to you is to build upon your relationship with them every single day, as the more positive they feel around you, the more likely they will be to listen to your guidance. You can influence your relationship with your child by spending time together, talking about their interests, participating in things they are interested in, and spending time laughing together. The activity itself is of little concern, if your child wishes to play video games with you, accept this invitation and have them teach you how to play alongside them. The purpose is to share quality time. Make jokes, partake in things they enjoy, and generally have a good time together.

Punish by Ignoring

This means systematically ignoring behaviors intended only to attract attention while reinforcing positive ones. This can be done with behaviors that do not create harm to people or property. Involve classmates, friends, teachers, daily caregivers, and expect the disturbing behavior to escalate at first (the child will try harder since he or she is not getting satisfaction).

The Scolding

This is a very important educational moment because it can provide the child with information about the right behavior. It should be addressed to the behavior and not to the child themself (it is a good rule never to use adjectival language "You are the usual bully, bad, absent-minded…" but "you kicked a girl and you hurt her, you have to understand that this is wrong…"), with a very firm and decisive tone, not abstemious and with a few words that say why the behavior is inappropriate: "you should have asked for the ball if you wanted it, so you wouldn't have hurt her and your teammates would have given it to you."

Create Safe Spaces for Everyone

When chaos ensues, it can become extremely stressful for everyone living under the same roof, even those not directly involved in the chaos. Chaos may not always consist of outbursts of anger or emotional meltdowns, but may instead be a challenging moment or a particularly difficult day filled with challenging sensations. Having a designated safe space for everyone in the home ensures that everyone has their area to retreat to if things become overwhelming. For your child, their bedroom might become their safe space. For you, your safe space may be your bedroom, office, or even the bathroom, so you can have a bath as you relax and unwind. Regardless of where they are, safe spaces should always be respected, and anytime someone is in their safe space, people should be particularly gentle and kind to that person as a way to show respect while they practice regulating their emotions.

Follow the Same Routine Every Day

Set up a routine for yourself and your child that you can follow every day, even on days off, and be sure to follow it. If you create a fun, easy-to-follow routine, it becomes enjoyable for your entire family to follow that routine, and you experience even more benefit from your routine. Since you need a routine that you can follow each day, it may be ideal to have a morning, afternoon, and bedtime routine that can be followed, while leaving room for adaptations during the rest of the day. This way, you can accommodate for the fact that things like school, work, errands, and leisurely tasks are often rotated during the daytime hours. You can also create routines around how specific tasks are done, such as getting ready for school or preparing to go out for leisurely activities, as this can help psychologically prepare your child for these activities, too.

Keep Promises You Make

Keeping your promises is so important because a promise gets your child's hopes up. No matter how big or small the promise is, you need to make sure you follow through with it. Things are not always going to go according to plan, but you still need to keep all of the promises you make. An easy way to avoid messing up as a parent is to not make any promises that you are unsure of. Many parents like to make promises to please their children but end up disappointing them in the end.

To avoid any broken promises, you need to have confidence and integrity. Make sure that you have realistic ways for yourself to follow through with what you are telling your child. See that you have a way to make this happen when you are promising it will. If you want to make a promise to a child, you can probably bet that they will ask you when it is going to happen, so be prepared to answer this question. If you do not know this answer yet, there are still likely some details that need to be sorted on your end. Broken promises create trust issues. You do not want your child to feel disappointed in you because the promise did not come true, so only make sure to make them on special occasions when you feel truly confident that they will happen. If you have control of the situation and can make it happen, then it should be safe for you to make a promise.

Recognize Positive Behaviors

Children with disorder explosions frequently require continuous feedback. Recognize what your child is doing well, even if it is only a tiny part of an immense task or something insignificant. For example, while most school-age children can dress and eat breakfast independently, many children with disorder explosions require praise for each step of the process to complete it on their own. Though many parents believe that they should not praise children for tasks expected of them at a certain age, explosive children require this praise to keep them motivated to complete these tasks independently. It may seem strange to praise children who are still developing skill sets that their peers have already incorporated—or that parents believe are simple—but it is necessary to keep disorder explosions children moving toward independence. Giant leaps can occur in unexpected time frames. Small changes happen all the time; be unconditionally supportive of your child and notice when they succeed, no matter how insignificant the accomplishment may appear to you.

Be Firm against Whining

All children whine sometimes, but this can become a very bad habit when it is not corrected. Make sure you put a policy in place that does not tolerate whining to get what they want. The first time that you enable this behavior, your child is going to run with it. They will see that whining is your weakness and that you are more willing to ultimately give in when they do it. Children are very smart in this way, and they know exactly how to push their buttons. Do not let this happen; stop it before it even starts. Remind yourself that giving in will just enable whatever it is that your child is trying to do to manipulate you. They might catch you in a moment of weakness or a moment when you simply feel too tired to argue. Whatever you do, make sure that you are not just giving in because it feels easier—there is always a better and more productive solution that you can use when you are raising your child. You are the parent, and it is up to you to maintain your role of authority.

Unplug Regularly

Studies have shown that excessive screen time or interaction with devices can increase behavioral issues in neurotypical children and adults, and can have an extremely detrimental impact on the wellbeing of children with behavioral disorders. Regularly unplugging your entire family from technology is an important approach to create more peace in your home by eliminating a known trigger from your life.

Do Things Together as a Family

Partaking in activities that are enjoyable for everyone involved is important to note. You should be mindful of anything that may trigger your child to avoid creating an overwhelming environment. Your plans may not always consist of extravagant trips to carnivals and movie theatres, so consider planning before even the simplest of activities such as; playing board games, growing your herb garden, kicking the football, baking a cake together, or even going for a walk at a nearby park.

Do what works for your family, and create space for your child to feel safe and comfortable. This time should not be about expanding their comfort zone or coping skills, but about enjoying a positive, peaceful time together as a family.

Maintain Composure with Mistakes

Mistakes or oversights are inevitable, no matter how hard you try to avoid them. Remaining composed through any of those slipups is an important aspect of maintaining peace, as it gives you the flexibility to navigate any upheavals with a calm and collected mindset. You might have noticed that, in the past, anytime a mistake presented itself, it seemed to spiral, and the day grew more and more stressful as time went by. This is because after one mistake was made, you remained on edge, expecting more problems to come out of that experience, and in turn, more chaos erupted.

When you perceive mistakes with a sense of grace, you deal with the mistake and trust that it was an isolated experience. Rather than anticipating further misfortune or bracing yourself for more chaos, you regain composure and work toward maintaining peace. As a result, you welcome a shift in perspective, and any upcoming obstacles can be faced with a relaxed state of calm and clarity.

Remaining Patient in the Moment

Forming a sense of patience for yourself in any present moment stems from understanding the entirety of the situation and preparing yourself for it in advance. Each day, prepare for the fact that you and your child will inevitably have a few challenging experiences, and create a productive mindset ahead of time that enables you through those challenges. This way, when you inevitably reach them, you are already at a point of understanding and patience in your mind, which means you are more likely to respond in such a manner, too.

Promoting a Problem-Solving Experience

After you have created space for patience and taken a moment for yourself, you need to promote an aptitude for problem-solving. This requires both you and your child to share interactions and conversations that promote a problem-solving environment. When you are both able to connect into a similar frame of mind and create a desire to solve the problem you are facing, it minimizes imminent outbursts while maximizing resolutions because you can address these situations head-on, together. This mindset is far more productive than any alternative, offering the greatest opportunity for you both to explore the situation in a positive, thorough manner. A major benefit of this approach to resolving problems is that you show your child that you are on their team and that you desire to find a solution together. When your child realizes they can rely on you and that you are insistent on helping them, rather than hindering them, they are likely to be more receptive to your approach.

Internally, focusing on problem-solving takes you out of the mindset of "what is wrong with us?" or "what is wrong with my child?" and allows you to instead focus on what can be done to form greater harmony at that moment. When you alternate your mindset, it becomes easier for you to lead yourself and your child into a more positive, productive atmosphere.

Within your child, focusing on problem-solving not only takes their attention off the trigger but also teaches them how to solve problems they may face in their lives. It is a common misconception that children with behavioral disorders are incapable of regulating themselves or solving their problems. They, like any child, are fully capable, however, the method in which they approach these skills or the amount of time it takes to successfully regulate themselves may differ. Teaching your child how to problem-solve using their unique reasoning, logic, and skills ensures that when they arrive at troubling situations, they have healthier coping methods for those situations. In the end, this proves to be a profound life experience for your child.

Genuinely Listening to Your Child's Needs

Children who experience defiant rages and intense meltdowns often struggle with the ability to control themselves because they do not adequately grasp what is going on internally. Their lack of understanding and inability to define those emotions impedes their capacity to appropriately express how they truly feel.

Actively listening to your child will welcome two refreshing benefits. The first benefit is that your child feels heard, and as an influence of feeling heard, you help them feel accepted. This state of acceptance demonstrates that they are irrefutably surrounded by people that care for them. Furthermore, providing a safe environment to articulate and express their emotions. Another advantage to taking in your child's input is that you can clearly understand how they are feeling, which means you can help your child correctly label their feelings and express those feelings more productively. For example, if your child is feeling irritated because things did not go their way, you can help them describe these feelings and recognize these feelings as being natural and safe to feel. You can also help them understand a more effective way of resolving those feelings of anger so they can completely express them without creating feelings of frustration, embarrassment, shame, or otherwise.

Genuinely listening to your child and his or her wishes is an eloquent means to quickly diffuse any situation, yet it is a commonly skipped step. It is a challenging, yet important initiative to remind yourself to slow down and listen when your own emotions running high. Patience is key here, as it encourages you to calm down and take the time to understand what your child is upset about. Once you have heard exactly what your child has to say, you can take relevant action to effectively diffuse the situation and move on more appropriately.

Be Consistent with Your Consequences

Delivering consequences to your child may seem difficult to follow through with. However, it is essential that if you promise a specific set of consequences to a child, you follow through on those consequences if they are disobeyed. Children with behavioral disorders will be far more likely to try to trigger your emotions and encourage you to cave to their preferences, and the minute they spot your weaknesses, they will seek to manipulate any vulnerabilities to get their way. This is not necessarily intentionally malicious but is ingrained as a part of their way of thinking.

Showing your child that there are indeed consequences and that those consequences will be followed through on every single occasion ensures that your child envisions your word as fact. Understand that children with behavioral disorders do not think like neurotypical children. About consequences, for example, a child with a behavioral disorder that believes there is a one in one-hundredth chance that a meltdown could help them get their way will commit to that meltdown. If you succumb to their ploys even just once, you encourage that meltdown to be a rewarding resolution every time, for they know that if they break you down hard enough, you will submit to their rule.

In no circumstance does this mean you should allow your child to harm themselves or someone else as you position your point across that they will not get their way, especially for poor behavior. However, you should not be afraid to let them cry or sort it out themselves, either. Let your child sit in their room and sort their emotions out for themselves. It may feel painful or overwhelming to you as their parent, but understand that this is an important part of your child's learning emotional self-regulation. Even though your child's ability to regulate their emotions may be inhibited, it does not mean it is entirely ruined. While your child's emotional dysregulation may differ from a neurotypical individual, a child with a behavioral disorder still grasps the capacity to regulate themselves, and they must discover their unique way of doing so. Help your child by providing a safe space to regulate within as they learn how to cope and manage their emotions.

Course Correct with Yourself First

If you find yourself amid a meltdown and cannot seem to position yourself or your child back on track, you need to stop and recall the importance of putting your safety mask on, first. Before you can help your child regulate themselves and steer away from intensifying outbursts, you have to address your emotional state. Reflect on your present thoughts while attempting to calm yourself down. Take a deep breath. Children no matter what age, will always heighten to match their parents' escalated state. This means if you are yelling, screaming, crying, or arguing with your child, you are inadvertently encouraging them to escalate their behavior, to match yours. If you have committed the mistake of engaging in a dispute, or if your anguish is causing heightened distress for your child, you need to stop and walk away from the situation. Relax your entire body and mind for a few moments while you compose yourself back into a grounded, calm state. Then, with a compassionate and peaceful approach, you can support your child in achieving the same sense of tranquility.

Upon recognizing the increasingly intensifying outburst, peacefully inform your child that you are walking away from this environment for a few minutes so you can calm yourself and address the situation in a more composed and productive manner. If possible, leave your child in a safe space such as their bedroom and have them wait there until you are ready to address the situation more respectfully. Then, as you stated remove yourself from the area and start the process of calming yourself down.

A child with a behavioral disorder like oppositional defiant disorder (ODD) will likely attempt to throw back in your face the fact that you already deviated away from the original behavioral plan. They may challenge your rationale with the use of guilt, embarrassment, or shame as a way to encourage you to feel deplorable about the deviance from the plan. The child will push fairly hard at this to pressure and manipulate you to reach their preferred outcome and get their way. You need to be aware of their tricks and prevent them from doing so by standing firm in your behavioral plan. Know that you are on the right track and that even if you had to course correct, you are making far more progress than you had in the past. Once you are done dealing with that particular situation, be sure to celebrate your success of rearranging things back on track, and allow yourself to release any undesirable emotions you may be holding onto. If you have someone you tend to talk to when things get out of control with your child or someone who is helping you improve the situation, now would be a great time to reach out to that person so you can obtain assistance. The calmer you become following a meltdown or a mistake, and the more perspective you accumulate, the easier it will be for you to view it as a positive experience regardless of what your child may have said. This way, you can go into the next experience with even more courage and confidence, and a greater ability to keep things from derailing. Please don't take what your child says to heart too much, understand they are just words and are being used in an attempt to assume control. You are doing great despite what anyone says. Over time, you and your child will be experiencing a far less dramatic approach to discipline and household rules!

CHAPTER 18
Build Your Child
Self-Esteem

One of the main sources of explosive child's self-esteem is the haters in the society who don't know anything about the disorder and yet, treat it as an untouchable thing. The reason behind this is the several misconceptions that are present in society.

Very often, you will find that skeptics make it clear that adults cannot have ADHD and that they are simply using it as an excuse to cover up their faults. They keep saying that whatever symptoms they are having or claim to have is because their parents did not hold the reins when they were young. They will tell you to deal with your shortcomings and grow up. But I have already given you plenty of evidence in this book to support the fact that disorder explosions are real. It is very real, and it happens in adults as well. So, if you do have to reply to the skeptics, do so with facts. One of the best ammunition you can produce in front of the skeptics of society is a hard fact. You can even take them to one of your meetings with your support group or send them articles that will educate them.

But if you are looking for something sarcastic, you can always tell them how nice it is for them to be smarter than some of the most renowned psychologists and scientists in the world.

Then comes another group of people who are best described as the crusaders. They will question every step you take and every decision you make. They will second guess your choice of doctor or even your medication. They might even tell you that disorder explosions medications are nothing but "kiddie cocaine," but then, you have to present them with facts that, like every other medication, disorder explosions meds have their side effects too. But that does not mean they are going to inculcate a feeling of dependency in the patient.

Before you go spouting off things to others, you need to make sure you have your facts straight. So, read as many articles as you can so that you can make an informed speech about how drug therapy is important for disorder explosions patients.

At the end of the day, you have to let go of what others think of you. You need to focus on yourself and your decisions. Ask yourself—do you want to take medications? Do medications make you feel better? Are you comfortable with taking medications? If the answer to these questions is yes, then who cares what others think? So, the next time someone comes to you with their holier-than-thou attitude about drug therapy, you can simply ask them would they deny taking insulin if they had been diagnosed with diabetes?

Then some people like to make sarcastic jokes about disorder explosions symptoms. They might say things like "If only I had disorder explosions, I could come up with some excuse for forgetting deadlines every month." When you protest, saying that these comments are disrespectful, they might say they were simply joking. The best way to deal with such people is to ignore them and not respond until the right moment comes. For example, if it is your boss who keeps humiliating you for your explosive disorder, you should avoid responding to those comments. Start looking for a new job, and when you find one, you can write a detailed report to the main office stating how your boss abused you just because of a medical condition. If you think you cannot put up with it any longer, you can use the direct approach and see how your boss responds. You can tell them that these comments are hurtful, and you'd like them not to continue being sarcastic. If this works, then it is okay; if it doesn't, then you have to wait for the right time to submit a written complaint.

The next type of people are the ones closest to us and yet fail to understand disorder explosions are a real problem. No matter how much evidence you provide them, they will not believe you. They might keep telling you that there is nothing wrong with you, and you are simply being lazy. Experts believe that family members often behave in such a manner because they cannot accept that anything like disorder explosions exists.

Moreover, they cannot accept that it might run in their family, so they go into denial. So, if you have someone like that in your family, you have to stand up to them and let them know that explosive disorder is a condition that you are suffering from, and it is not about them. In the beginning, it might be difficult, but as time passes, these types of people will give up.

Disorder explosions can make it difficult to concentrate. As a result, if your child has disorder explosions, he or she is more likely to receive poor grades, suspensions, or detentions. They may also have poor social skills and be rejected by their peers.

Parents, relatives, and other authority figures, such as teachers and caretakers, may lose patience with them, become upset, and attempt to criticize and "correct" their conduct.

"There is much negative feedback coming from all of these various ways, and they internalize it and start to feel pretty awful about themselves."

According to several studies, when children with disorder explosions mature into adults, their self-esteem continues to erode over time due to increasing criticism and complex life events.

Children's Self Esteem

Growing up with disorder explosions can cause self-esteem issues, making it difficult to take acceptable risks in relationships and friendships, careers, education, and the workplace. Without taking those chances, further progress may be restricted or nonexistent.

According to clinic doctors, "when you have strong self-esteem, you feel pretty good for yourself and regard yourself as deserving of others' respect." "When you have poor self-esteem, you do not respect your thoughts and opinions. You could be concerned that you are not good enough all of the time."

Rather than viewing explosive disorder as a personal fault, we must help others to enhance their self-esteem by concentrating on learning strategies to be successful with their symptoms. With younger kids, one should typically avoid using "disorder explosions," leaving it up to their parents. Instead, it challenges students to come up with a term for the brain type they possess.

"They give their brain a label based on how they feel disorder explosions," Call it attention-wandering or quick brain in the workplace. 'You have a highly creative brain,' you may add. You are thinking about a lot of things simultaneously. We are calling it a 'many ideas brain.'"

While teenagers may feel relieved, many are still concerned that disorder explosions may separate them from their peers or hinder them from reaching their objectives. We must assist children in identifying role models with an explosive disorder, such as Michael Phelps or Simone Biles.

"The aim is to accept and deal with the brain that you have."

For every harmful statement, children need to receive three nice or encouraging ones. A poll was conducted just like an informal survey to see how many negative remarks a kid or teen hears in comparison to good comments. According to estimation, for every 15 negative remarks, a child having disorder explosions receives, just one good comment.

"You internalize that voice if you hear the message that you are missing the point over and over again as a kid," Imagine how that affects someone's self-assurance.

Parents can do much to help their children overcome their low self-esteem.

Referring to the method as the 5 Cs of parenting:

- **Self-control:** First and foremost, learn to regulate your own emotions so you can behave successfully and teach your kids to do the same.
- **Compassion:** Accept your child for who they are, not who you think they should be.
- **Collaboration:** Instead of forcing your rules on the kid and co-parent, work together to discover answers to daily difficulties.
- **Consistency:** Maintain consistency by doing what you say you will do again and over again.
- **Celebration:** Recognize what works and do more of it day after day.

"Celebration is truly noticing." "It is recognizing and validating the good developments you observe. You may boost their self-esteem by recognizing and validating both their accomplishments and efforts. You are fostering their tenacity and self-assurance."

When a disorder explosions diagnosis is eventually made, it should provide a chance to analyze the past better and then put in place the behavioral and academic assistance that will help in the future. Providing opportunities for achievement can allow a kid or teen's self-esteem to be rebuilt and strengthened.

"Learning how to do this and skills, as well as the emotions of coping with it," is one of the essential things after a disorder explosions diagnosis.

How can you identify if your child is having issues with his or her self-esteem?

"A huge indication is that they regularly make critical comments about one, even after small mistakes."

They may refuse to try something new, even though they have in the past. This might indicate that they do not believe they are "competent or talented enough to thrive in new hobbies."

They may say things like, "Well, I am not a great student, then why should I try any longer?"

They may also ignore or minimize some possibilities,

claiming, "It is dumb anyhow," since they are unsure of their capacity to thrive. Furthermore, they could be gloomy about alternative possibilities.

They may distance from friends or family, lose interest in things they formerly enjoyed, experience an increased or reduced appetite (not related to developmental changes such as growth spurts or puberty), receive poorer grades, or lose friends.

Different Ways to Safeguard a Child's Self Esteem

Praise your child for accomplishments while also acknowledging and mentioning the obstacles that made it difficult for your kid to do so.

Negative criticism regularly might damage your child's self-esteem. Recognize your child's accomplishments, no matter how minor they may be. Make an effort to observe when your kid is paying attention or doing what he is meant to be doing—and what discipline and skills he used to get there.

Tell your child what he did great—not just a generic "good work!" but something specific like "I love how you thought about the task and organized your outline!" This will not only boost your child's self-esteem but will also reinforce his grasp of what it takes to thrive so he can repeat the process. This can also educate him to appreciate small victories instead of being overly harsh on himself.

Encourage your children to understand that everyone makes mistakes, and the essential thing is to learn from them rather than dwell on them. Confident individuals do not let fear of failure stop them from succeeding—not because they are certain they will never fail, but rather because they learned how to cope with setbacks.

Describe any mental or emotional obstacles he had to face to get ahead in this situation. Just an example that, "You understand that other ideas sidetracked him, but he or she fought hard to overcome them and stay on track. "Congratulations!"

Disorder explosions frequently give "mirror characteristics" that are pretty valuable. Recognize your child's assets. She may not be a great reader, but she has the potential to be the next Picasso. He might not be great at writing reports, but he has an uncanny ability to come up with innovative new ideas. Recognize, reward, and capitalize on your child's skills so that he or she feels proud and accomplished.

Recognize that they may be experiencing lingering anxiousness after school and that he requires time to "wind down" by doing something he enjoys. Make that dynamic explicit so that they learn to understand their own emotions and how to cope with and conquer them.

Ascertain that your child has the potential to thrive while participating in these hobbies and that untreated disorder explosion does not harm their abilities. Also, do not ruin the enjoyment by depriving them of activities they enjoy as a "prize" for performing the ones they dislikes.

Setting and accomplishing objectives, big and little, makes children feel powerful. Encourage your kid to develop a list of things they want to do to help them transform their ambitions and dreams into practical objectives. After that, practice breaking down relatively long goals into manageable milestones. You will be recognizing their passions and assisting them in developing the abilities they will need to achieve their life objectives.

Break down difficult jobs into tiny incremental steps or components to assist your youngster in completing them. Recognize their successes at each stage; this will boost their confidence, motivate them to take the next step and teach them how to break down projects into manageable sub-tasks—and organizing skills.

Many youngsters may use their rooms as "horizontal storage" for their toys, covering each inch of the floor. Sit down with your youngster and walk him through each category of cleaning one at a time. "Where are all the red trucks going?" "Great! Where are all the blue vehicles going now?" "You loved how they painstakingly sorted the toys into categories—now you will know where it all belongs!" say once it is all done.

Make a special time for both you and your child every day. A special occasion, whether it is an outing, playing games, or simply spending time with your kid in good interaction, may assist in strengthening your child's self-worth. It also promotes healthy attachment; studies have shown that insecure connection is linked to disorder explosions and impedes the development of a good self-image.

With your youngster, practice social skills. Because of their hyperactive, impulsive, or violent actions, children with disorder explosions may be shunned by their classmates. Play role-playing games with your youngster in a variety of social situations. Ask them to imagine how a buddy, for example, might react if they did certain things or acted in a certain manner. Request that your youngster act it out. Then urge them to envision an alternate way of acting that would not anger or irritate their friend. Choose one-word "codes" or "signals" to indicate each desired action. Invite one of their peers over for a supervised play session, and call out the applicable code words as needed to encourage your kid to choose the more successful action they demonstrated.

Assure your child that you will always support and love them. There will be moments when you are tired, angry, or anxious, and it will be difficult to love. Recognize such moments and give yourself permission to take a deep breath and consider how your kid is feeling. This is when it is even more critical that you recognize and show your love for your child's ongoing challenges. Let your kid know that you'll be there for them through both good and bad times.

Protecting Their Self-Esteem While Helping Them Grow

There is another extremely important part of training explosive children, and that is encouragement. After all, your goal is not to just get them to master a task but to get them to feel good about mastering it. One of the most damaging parts of anyone's psychological state is when words are used in the wrong way.

Some parents, out of frustration will use force, ultimatums, and punishments to intimidate the child into better behavior. These types of actions are often based on the idea that the child is being deliberately rebellious and willful. As we've already learned, this is not the case with explosive children. While punishment may be warranted from time to time, it is not the most effective way to teach. The focus is on the bad behavior and not the positive. It doesn't address the issue of teaching the child correct behavior but instead concentrates on teaching them what not to do. Add to that the fact that harsh words are painful and when they come from someone they are relying on getting them through life it is especially difficult to hear. In time, it drives a wedge between you two, one that continues to grow to separate you more and more each time they are shared. Eventually, you could find yourself separated from your child by a deep chasm that may be nearly impossible to overcome.

The best solution, therefore, is to your positive praise and encouragement to guide your child in the right direction. Praise given can do wonders for your child's self-esteem if done correctly. The easy way is to say words like, "good job," "that's awesome," or "I'm so proud of you." These are wonderful ways to start a positive dialogue with your child. However, studies have shown that when you are more specific, the praise yields the best results. Instead of "good job," try something like, "I like the way you came in and started your homework right away, good job!" Now the child knows exactly what they are being praised for.

Even when you give praise, you have to be careful how you do it. Maybe you've seen those parents who mix praise and criticism. "You did a really good job washing the dishes, why can't you do that all the time?" This kind of praise often confuses and frustrates the child rather than reinforces the spirit. At best, it reduces the power that your positive words are trying to say. Next are a few basic guidelines that can teach you how to give appropriate praise to your child when needed.

Teach Yourself to Pay Positive Attention

It may sound strange to tell a parent that they need to learn how to pay attention to their child, but that's exactly what's needed at times. Parents are often busy with affairs and forget to set aside one on one time with their children. Try to block out a time when it is just you and the child and observe them. Don't hover over them like a mother hen but let them move about freely in their activity and watch what they are doing. If they are playing a game, don't jump in right at the beginning but sit back and watch for a while. Once you understand what they are doing narrate their actions back to the child, so they understand. This works better when you show a little enthusiasm in your descriptions. Match your enthusiasm to the age of the child. Younger children enjoy more animation, but you can tone it down as they get older.

As you speak, give them both verbal and non-verbal signs of approval when you see them doing something you like.

Non-verbal signs could include a hug, wrapping your arm around them, a pat on the head, a soft rub on the shoulder, a high-five, a smile, a wink, etc. Verbal skills could mean saying things like "I like it when you do…" Or "that is so grown up when you do…"

You can also praise progress. "Last year you couldn't do…

But now look at you."

If during your time together, the kid misbehaves, turn your attention away and focus on something else. That usually works to get the child to adjust their conduct. If the bad behavior persists, tell them that your time together is over and that you'll spend time again when they can control their behavior.

Be Clear in Your Commands

When giving a command to your child, the compliance begins with you. Never give a command that you do not genuinely expect them to do. Back up every request with the reward or consequences outlined.

Do not make it in the form of a question as this can give them the idea that obedience is optional. Do not say, "why don't you get ready for bed now?" rather make it direct, "get ready for bed." When you raise your inflection at the end of the sentence, children will subconsciously believe that you are asking them if they want to get ready for bed. Make sure your tone is clear enough to let them know you expect compliance.

You also want to make sure your child is listening to you. Eliminate all distractions that could divert their attention, and ask them to repeat the command, so you know they heard it and understood.

Teach Your Child Not to Interrupt

Children crave attention and will do anything to get it. If you give a lot of attention to a child that interrupts, you can expect to continue to have a parade of interruptions. To avoid this problem, before you are engaged in any type of activity like talking to a neighbor or on the phone give them a command to do something that will keep them occupied while you are otherwise engaged.

Make sure that the task you ask them to do is something they will enjoy. If the child obeys your instructions, stop what you're doing for a second to give them praise. Continue to do this every few minutes until you finish your activity. As the child becomes accustomed to this type of instruction and praise, you can extend the time between praises to keep them engaged.

If they look as if they're going to interrupt you, stop and give them praise for obeying what they're doing and then refocus their attention on the task you want them to do.

In the end, make sure you praise or reward the child for following your instructions before you go on to another activity.

Use Constructive Punishment

When children become defiant or disobey, it is important

to remember that it is not that they are refusing to follow your commands. Outright defiance is not a characteristic of disorder explosions. What is happening is that their lack of executive skills often pulls them away mentally from whatever task you've assigned. It could be that the task is very boring or very hard, which can be very uncomfortable for them.

Punishment, however, should be used as a last resort. It is better to find a more positive and self-edifying means of praise and incentives to motivate the child. There are several ways to punish a child in a way that helps them get the point.

Fines: If you used the reward system to motivate them you could also use the fine system to remove privileges. For example, if they receive 5 tokens for obeying your directives you can choose to deduct tokens for disobedience.

Manage Your Child in Public Places

The secret to getting your child to be obedient in public lies in the preparation. Make sure they know what's expected of them before you go out. Give them a short list of rules to follow and make sure they understand them. Have them repeat them back to you, so he owns the instructions. Review the instructions before you go in and if they disobey take them out to your car and wait until they are ready to try again.

Establish an incentive to motivate them to obey your directives and punishment if they disobey.

Keep them busy. Give them an activity that they enjoy keeping them occupied. It is a good idea to have several ready to go so you can keep them engaged while you are out.

No matter which methods you use to manage your child's behavior whether in public or at home they should be used consistently so as not to confuse the child. It will not be an easy ride, but if you are consistent, there is real hope that in the end your child will respond and grow from the experience. While it is easier said than done, never take a child's behavior personally or to the point that you forget you're working with a child with a disability. Learn the art of forgiveness for both your child and for yourself, and you'll both be happy about it.

How to Help Disorder Explosions Children Make Friends

Building Friendship Growth Opportunities

For elementary and preschool children, playdates offer a great opportunity for parents to model and coach positive peer interactions for them. For the child, they would be able to practice these new skills. You can set up these playtimes with 1–2 friends at a time—keep it minimal rather than having a large group of friends as this may be overwhelming for the child and you. Plan playtime to be the most effective for your child.

Consider yourself as your child's "friendship mentor." Consider carefully how long a playdate takes and select activities that are most interesting for your child.

The older the child gets, friendships and peer relationships become more complicated but continue to remain involved in your child's life and help them facilitate interactions that are positive for themselves. For a kid who struggles socially, middle and high school years can be harsh. It would be good if the child can have a least 1–2 good friends throughout the years of school that can often be the child's support system rather than having a large group of friends.

Socially alienated middle-or secondary school students who face constant rejection may feel desperate to become members of any peer group—including those with adverse impact.

Another way to foster positive peer relationships outside of school is to get involved in groups within the community such as Indian Guides, Boy Scouts, Girl Scouts, Girls Who Code, Rotary Club for kids, sports teams, and art groups, for example. When getting your children to join these clubs and teams, ensure that group leaders or mentors know about disorder explosions and create an environment that is both encouraging and constructive for your child. This is extremely helpful in the long run.

Don't be worried or afraid to share information about your child's condition with kindergarten, coaches, and parents in the community so you know what's going on with your child and who's spending time with your child. Withholding information will only make things worse. The peer group of a child and the features of the group affect the individuals in the group strongly.

Empowering the Peer Status of Your Child through School

Peer groups are important for children, but the downside is that once they put a label on your child because of their lack of social skills, it can be hard to break away from this reputation. Having a reputation, especially one that isn't "cool," can become an obstacle for your child. Negative peer labels are commonly established when the child is in early to middle school and this reputation does not fade away easily, even though the child develops positive social skills. This is one of the main reasons why it is extremely crucial for parents to collaborate with the school and their child's teachers, mentors, and coaches to address any effects.

Lessening or stopping these negative impacts can be done through establishing a positive working relationship with your child—this is just one such example. Inform them about the strengths and desires of your child as well as what they struggle with. You can also share any approaches that you find helpful in focusing on the areas of weakness of your child.

When forming social preferences about their peers, young children often look to their teacher. A teacher's presence, warmth, acceptance, patience, and gentle direction can be an excellent model for the peer group and it also influences the child's social status. The teacher plays an important role in finding other ways to draw positive attention to the disorder explosions child.

In the presence of the other children in the school, one way to do this is to give the child special roles and obligations. As a teacher, you can make sure that these responsibilities can result in the child feeling success, and this can, in turn, develop feelings of acceptance within the classroom as well as feelings of confidence, self-esteem, and self-worth in the self-conscious child.

This also gives opportunities for the peer group to view the child in a positive and encouraging light, which also helps to stop the group process of peer rejection. It can also help to promote social acceptance by pairing the child with a caring "buddy" in the classroom.

Setting Up Accommodations in School and at Home

The benefits of having a good, working relationship with your child's teacher are enabling them or helping the teacher outfit disorder explosions techniques and methods in the classroom. This helps the child to manage their symptoms better. Working together with a teacher or an adult caregiver, therapist, or coach on effective approaches towards behavior management and social skills is the best and most practical solution.

Inform your child's teacher about the medication taken by your child and if they need to take it during school hours. Be sure to work closely with the child's doctor as well because you may need to give feedback on your child's responses, symptoms, and so on both at home and school, so the doctor would be able to fine-tune and make adjustments to the child's medication along the way.

CHAPTER 19

GAMES FOR
EXPLOSIVE KIDS

Water Color Painting

Once your toddler reaches 24–30 months old, he or she starts recognizing and appreciating colors. It is, therefore, fitting for toddlers to be exposed to painting activities. The materials needed for painting are cheap and readily available in stores so it will not be difficult for parents to set up a small corner or outdoor area for painting.

Before you leave your child to paint on their own, make sure to establish clear rules. First, demonstrate how to properly handle the materials. Second, show your child where to hang their finished painting. Lastly, show your child how to clean up after. Take note all these demonstrations are just done through modeling. You do not even need to speak a single word. Just show your child how it is done.

Playing Musical Instruments

While most activities are performed with either the left or right side of the brain, music engages both sides of the brain, strengthening your child's ability to multitask.

If your child is musically gifted, encourage them by signing them up for lessons, investing in the instrument of their choice, or whatever else they need to pursue their passion. Singing groups, orchestras, and choirs are also an excellent way for your child to improve social skills and make like-minded friends.

Aside from the interest in colors, older toddlers are very sensitive to musical notes which makes it the perfect time for them to be introduced to different musical instruments. Some child-friendly instruments are child-sized organs, tambourines, mini-guitars, and mini-drums.

Similar to how you introduced painting to your child, make sure you demonstrated well the proper usage and storage of the instruments. Show how to gently press the keys, gently strum the strings, or gently tap the tambourine to not create a loud noise. Keep everything orderly and manageable.

Once your child knows how to properly use the instruments and how to properly stow them away, let them play the music that they want. Even if it sounds incoherent to you, for your child it is already a good melody. Prevent yourself from correcting your child except when they mishandle the material, instead give praises when they do the activity in an orderly fashion.

Individual Sports

Your child may find team sports challenging because of their disorder explosions symptoms, so you might want to consider individual sports instead of helping your child succeed better.

If your child is a sports lover, they have dozens of exciting and enjoyable individual sports to choose from, such as:

- Martial arts
- Tennis
- Wrestling
- Swimming
- Bowling
- Fencing
- Table tennis
- Skateboarding
- Roller-skating
- Ice skating
- Track and field

Your child's natural high energy and enthusiasm will help them succeed in these types of sports and even become a champion!

Likewise, if you feel that your child's abilities are perfect for a particular sport, again, don't pressure them if the sport isn't appealing to them. Let your child suggest and choose.

Whatever individual sport your child chooses to practice, it will be a perfect outlet for their energy. IT will help keep disorder explosions symptoms in control, help them focus better, develop social skills, and sleep better.

Indoor Activities

When the weather doesn't allow for outdoor activities, you need to have various indoor activities to keep your child occupied and give them an outlet for their energy. Ideally, indoor activities should follow these basic rules:

Indoor Activities for Kids with Disorder Explosions Need to Be Structured

Those kids crave structure. They need to know what will follow, what to expect, and how they are supposed to act in each situation.

What will I do? Where will I be? What is okay for me to say or do?

You need to provide that structure for them in the form of structured activities. That means telling your child what he or she has to do, providing the required materials, and making it clear what they need to do to win or succeed. An example is telling the child to color in a whole page of a coloring book using three colors.

Indoor Activities Should Involve as Many Senses as Possible

In the above example, you have engaged the child's sense of touch and sight.

Multisensory activities help the child focus better. Some multisensory activities include:

- Cooking
- Board games
- Card games
- Building with Legos
- Hula hooping
- Coloring and painting
- Play Dough
- Twister
- Jumping rope
- Balloon volleyball

Indoor Activities Should Involve Movement

Of course, this is not always possible with all games. Gauge your child's energy and mood and decide whether you need to structure the activity with more (or less) movement. Or, combine activities with more dancing activities, with quieter activities like board games or video games. Remember to structure time for these activities as well.

Indoor Activities Can Be Group Activities or Individual Activities and Activities with More Movement and Quieter Ones

Here are some more suggestions:

- Hide and seek
- Dancing
- Charades
- Baking cookies
- Building

- Listening to audiobooks
- Crafts
- Scavenger hunts
- Singing
- Obstacle course
- Tramp lining

Now that you get the idea, go ahead and come up with some activities of your own to ensure that your child stays active and engaged on those rainy days!

Play Therapy

Play therapy is a fantastic tool. It is used in many psychotherapy and child psychology areas to help children with disorders develop skills while having fun.

You may choose to have your child engage in play therapy with a specialized child psychologist; however, you can easily use this method with your child at home as well.

Art Therapy

This type of therapy helps children develop their creative talents and express themselves through art. The child is asked to make a painting or drawing, describe their day at school, or an enjoyable event, something they like, or even draw themselves as they feel.

The child's artwork may uncover specific issues that he or she is having, allowing parents or the therapist to discuss them further. Besides, it's just a great way to keep the child focused while exploring and developing their creativity and uniqueness. Here are some suggestions:

- Making a collage with old photos or pictures from magazines.
- Designing a postcard with a short message to someone the child is angry with or wants to thank.
- Making a digital slide show with photos that make the child happy (or sad)
- Responding to music; listening to a short piece of music and drawing how it makes the child feel.
- Decorate a window with window markers
- Write a message to a balloon and send it flying away.
- Finger painting
- Drawing a self-portrait
- Making a drawing for someone special
- Drawing with eyes closed

The more challenging forms of exercise result in better brain function. Jujitsu, taekwondo, judo, karate, and other similar martial arts sports challenge both mind and bodywork very well for children with disorder explosions. They teach your child to focus and concentrate. They sharpen memory through their series of actions. They help develop excellent motor skills. They teach timing and balance. They also help your child realize that actions have consequences.

Other forms of exercise that have benefits similar to those of martial arts include dance, yoga, gymnastics, and rock climbing.

Fantasy Play

Children with disorder explosions often have trouble expressing and channeling their emotions. Fantasy play is crucial for teaching kids with disorder explosions how to express themselves better when feeling angry or frustrated.

How to structure play therapy?

Set fixed times. Play sessions should be between 10 to 15 minutes so that the child does not get bored; however, if the child retains an interest in the game for longer than that, allows him or her to continue.

Prompt the child while playing. For example, if you are playing with a puppet named Fred, start the game by saying, "One day as Fred was walking to school…" or "Once upon a time, there was…" During the game, you can also prompt your child by playing a role in the game.

Encourage good social behavior during the game. For example, "What will happen if the doctor shouts at the sick person?" or "How will the little girl feel if her friend doesn't want to share?"

Some suggestions of fantasy play are:

- Playing with dolls
- Doctor kits
- Han and finger puppets
- Stuffed animals
- Action figures and monster figures

Learning Life Skills

These skills are crucial to developing at this age as they will remain with your child for life. They include learning to handle frustration and anger, wait their turn, and finish assigned tasks. Games that help build social skills include:

- Let's Go Fish
- The Memory Game
- Chutes and Ladders
- Chinese Checkers
- Clue
- Role-playing with costumes or masks
- Playing with action figures
- Mock tea parties

Play therapy for older kids:

- Strategy video games
- Time management video games
- Superhero role play

- Art therapy

Brain Games

Researchers from Kennesaw State University and Augusta State University in the U.S. have shown that brain games can be a new form of disorder explosions therapy. Brain games stimulate the prefrontal cortex of the brain and help explosive children overcome distractions. The study suggested that brain games could be an alternative to medication. Following studies have concluded that brain games work to develop the brain, improve focus and attention, and help disorder explosions kids learn better. The ongoing research is very promising.

Following these findings, dozens of "brain training" programs have emerged, many of them making huge claims that are not backed up by science. My advice is to beware of these programs and stick to traditional brain games like puzzles, riddles, and brain teasers. Do not shell out money to a bogus program.

Brain games benefit children with disorder explosions by:

- Strengthening memory
- Developing problem-solving skills.
- Enhancing logical thinking and deduction skills
- Improving concentration

- Promoting pattern recognition
- Video brain games improve visual perception and spatial recognition.
- Enhancing cognitive skills.
- Enhancing reasoning skills.

Brain games help children learn these skills by having fun, which is always the best way to learn. Therefore, it makes total sense to schedule these types of games into your child's activities.

Here are some good suggestions:

- Brainteaser eBooks.
- Brainteaser websites
- Riddle eBooks
- Video brain games
- Crossword puzzle books
- Logic problem books
- Brain game apps. There is a variety to choose from suitable for all ages.
- Additional activities and fun games

Coloring Books

Coloring books have been around since our grandparents' time and are generally overlooked in today's digital era. However, the benefits of coloring for your explosive child should not be ignored. Children are never too old to color, and in fact, paint has been shown to relieve stress in adults! The benefits include:

- Preparing preschoolers for school
- Improving motor skills
- Developing good handwriting
- Enhancing creativity
- Developing awareness of colors
- Improving focus
- Improving hand-eye coordination
- Enhancing confidence when kids are praised for their work.
- Developing self-expression skills.

Drama

If your child loves to act and has the talent, drama groups and classes will benefit them immensely. They will have to focus on memorizing lines and learning to interact with others in a group effort within a structured environment. To top it all off, the applause at the end of the show is just the kind of praise and encouragement he needs!

Debate Teams

That could be a very fun learning experience for your teen. It will sharpen his communication and social skills, challenge their intellect, and showcase their natural enthusiasm and passion. It can also lower their stress level and bring out their best self. Join a local, state or the national debate team. The majority of debate programs are student-run and student-operated. As a team, they will have to follow the debate rules. They are familiar with making directed speeches to a large audience. They write and share their prepared speeches. They are used to being creative and are sometimes even artistic in their speech delivery and argument style.

Playground and Obstacle Games

Bringing your toddler to the playground is one way to take away their home boredom. Introduce your toddler to the various obstacle games present in the park or playground nearby. Always demonstrate how to perform such courses for safety. Let your toddler experience the tire game or the balance beam, but of course with your close supervision. Let your child experience other obstacles courses as crawling under arcs and the like. This will not only improve your child's physical strength, but it will also improve his/her thinking skills as well as his/her patience and determination.

Outdoor Chores

Toddlers love to sweep. You will be surprised by how much patience and exactness they have in using the broom and the dustpan. If you have a huge lawn with dried leaves, bring your child out to the yard and demonstrate how to sweep the dried leaves. After a few demonstrations, give your child a child-sized broom and dustpan and you'll enjoy your toddler go.

The first 5 steps in transforming an explosive toddler into a calm one are long-term solutions as well as forward-thinking remedies to temper tantrums. These 2 steps do not wait for the toddler to throw a fit; instead, it helps prevent the frequency of tantrum episodes. Since these two steps are long-term solutions, their implementation requires time and consistency as well. With enough patience and love, both steps will reap rewards in the future and will help reveal a calmer toddler sooner than you think.

The remaining 2 steps to transforming an explosive toddler to a calm one are more short-term and will show immediate results. Even if it has short-term effects, all steps must still be carried out consistently so your toddler will know what to expect every time he or she throws a tantrum.

Assume you are trapped within a video game, where everybody is coming at you simultaneously. Every sound, sight, and sensation serves as a deterrent. Getting through a regular day for a youngster with disorder explosions is similar to that. It also explains a lot about how they perceive the world.

Lack of concentration, impairment of functions like impulse control, memory, processing speed, and the good at following directions are common symptoms of disorder explosions in children.

For years, it was assumed that all of us were born with an abundance of brain cells; but we have been unable to generate more or modify how those cells functioned. Neuroscientists have found the presence of a phenomenon known as neuroplasticity, which allows the brain to create new cells or change the functioning of existing cells.

Cognitive exercises or games have been shown to generate desirable changes in how the brain functions and appears. This implies that parents may now work with their children to assist them in improving their explosive disorder symptoms.

To get you started, here are a few basic games.

The Memory Game

This game is really simple yet extremely effective. It significantly improves the memory and attention span of children with disorder explosions. The memory cards are arranged face down on the table. The first player takes two cards and tries to match them. If the cards do not match, the player must reshuffle the deck and place it face down. To recall where the card was put, the kids must keep their attention on the cards at all times.

Chutes and Ladders

This game is not only entertaining to play, but it also teaches vital lessons about predicting success and dealing with loss. The game's goal is for the players to proceed along a path that leads to the top of the playing board. You climb ladders (the success part), and if you fail, then chutes slide down along the route. When the children have to slide down on the chute, they become agitated, but they immediately realize a ladder nearby. Failure leads to success—this game teaches valuable life lessons.

Hoot Owl Hoot

This game is primarily about forming bonds with your teammates. Hoot Owl Hoot's goal is to get all owls back to their nests well before the sun rises. It is a battle with the sun. The players take turns choosing cards and deciding what steps they should take. Each action has a rationale, demonstrating that executive functioning abilities are honed throughout the game.

Battleship

Battleship is a strategic board game in which one player attempts to sink the ships of the opponent. This board game is fantastic for disorder explosions kids since it teaches them how to think logically and reason. It exposes kids to grids and coordinates, which incorporate basic arithmetic concepts.

Chess

Chess has long become one of the most popular disorder explosions games and one of the finest games for concentration. It not only improves attention but also helps to enhance strategic thinking abilities. You can play it as a board game. The main goal of the game is to checkmate your opponent. It is played on an 8x8 grid with each opponent having 1 Queen, 1 King, 2 Bishops, 2 Rooks, 2 Knights, and 8 Pawns. Each piece moves distinctly; chess pieces are generally black and white, and white always moves first.

Sudoku

There are several stages of difficulty in the game. According to these levels, the game will begin with numbers that have already been put in the grid. Not only does this game increase attention, but it also helps with math, focus, concentration, learning, and memory. So, if you are searching for activities to help explosive children enhance their focus, try Sudoku.

CONCLUSION

Thank you for reading this book. You now know what you must do now to help your child live a healthy and happy life, and this is such a great feeling to have as a constantly worried parent. Take each lesson that you have learned, and use it until it no longer applies. Most of these methods and strategies are lifelong skills that will be useful even when your child becomes an adult. What you teach them now is going to benefit them for a very long time, and it will encourage them to develop their coping skills. By understanding exactly what disorder explosions are and how to recognize them, you are giving your child a chance to live a normal life.

As a parent, it is your job to learn as much as you can about the disorder. By educating yourself, you are giving yourself the power to educate others. Working with their teachers, other children, and loved ones in your life, you should be able to create a great environment for your child no matter where they are. This is what matters most, and this is what will help them to succeed. Your child needs stability and consistency because disorder explosions often try to take this away from them at any chance it gets.

No matter what your child wants to be when they grow up, they can accomplish anything they set their mind on despite their disorder explosions. With the right guidance and access to coping skills and treatment from a young age, you will find that your child will grow up with the confidence necessary to succeed. You will also be able to feel proud of yourself as a parent for being the pillar of strength that they needed to get through this crazy journey that is life.

The techniques, methods, therapy, and treatments discussed in this book, it is all done to ensure that you get the right information and knowledge to guide you into making the right decisions for your child.

No matter what phase you are in the explosive disorder treatment or diagnosis, remember that you must always keep yourself informed, knowing what the disorder is, is the key element in providing the right assistance to your child, to yourself, to your spouse, and even to the teacher teaching your child.

Help and support, whether mentally, financially, physically support even are there when you know where to look. As parents, getting emotional and mental support from other parents is also crucial to enable you to have the strength to carry on at times when dealing with a disorder explosions child may seem to be overwhelming.

You must start practicing all of the techniques taught in this book consistently, as consistency is crucial to your ability to teach your child new habits. Your consistency will also help both yourself and your child recognize these techniques as being positive and useful tools, encouraging far more positive responses to them over time. Before you know it, you will both anticipate the positive side effects of your changed approach, empowering your child to push through and positively navigate any struggles.

I encourage you to always keep learning about your child and their needs and to continue implementing peaceful practices as often as possible. In doing so, you will drastically improve your quality of life, and the quality of life of your child, too.

Good luck.

REFERENCES

Food Com. (n.d.). *5 Healthy Lunches for Kids*. https://www.foodnetwork.com/healthy/photos/5-healthy-lunches-for-kids.

ADDitude. (2021, February 5). *Change Your Diet, Find Your Focus*. https://www.additudemag.com/can-the-right-diet-ease-add-symptoms/.

ADDitude. (2021, March 8). *"None of Us Were Trained How to Be Good Parents:" An ADHD Guide to Behavior Therapy*. https://www.additudemag.com/using-behavior-therapy-with-your-child/.

ADHD Parenting Tips. HelpGuide.org. (2021, April 19). https://www.helpguide.org/articles/add-adhd/when-your-child-has-attention-deficit-disorder-adhd.htm.

American Psychiatric Association. (2021). What Is Obsessive-Compulsive Disorder? Psychiatry.org. https://www.psychiatry.org/patients-families/ocd/what-is-obsessive-compulsive-disorder.

Arns, M., de Ridder, S., Strehl, U., Breteler, M. and Coenen, A. (2009). Efficacy of Neurofeedback Treatment in ADHD: The Effects on Inattention, Impulsivity, and Hyperactivity: A Meta-Analysis. Clinical EEG and Neuroscience, 40(3), pp.180-189.

Arnold, L., Lofthouse, N. and Hurt, E. (2012). Artificial Food Colors and Attention-Deficit/Hyperactivity Symptoms: Conclusions to Dye For. Neurotherapeutics, 9(3), pp.599-609.

Barkley, R. (1997, November 30). *Your Defiant Child: 8 Steps to Better Behavior*. ERIC. https://eric.ed.gov/?id=ED426763.

Bhandari, S. (2021, April 21). *Ways to Help Your Child With ADHD Succeed at School*. WebMD. https://www.webmd.com/add-adhd/childhood-adhd/adhd-how-to-help-your-child-succeed-at-school.

Carpenter, D. (2021, April 30). *Never Punish a Child for Bad Behavior Outside Their Control*. ADDitude. https://www.additudemag.com/behavior-punishment-parenting-child-with-adhd/.

Centers for Disease Control and Prevention. (2020, September 21). *Symptoms and Diagnosis of ADHD*. Centers for Disease Control and Prevention. https://www.cdc.gov/ncbddd/adhd/diagnosis.html.

Dodson, W. (2021, March 18). *What Is ADHD? Meaning, Symptoms & Amp; Tests*. ADDitude. https://www.additudemag.com/what-is-adhd-symptoms-causes-treatments/.

Edelman, G. (2021, March 30). *How to Make Friends: A Guide for Kids With ADHD (and Their Parents, Too)*. ADDitude. https://www.additudemag.com/how-to-make-friends-a-guide-for-kids-with-adhd/.

Raising Children Network. (2020, September 24). *Encouraging Good Behavior: 15 Tips*. https://raisingchildren.net.au/toddlers/behaviour/encouraging-good-behaviour/good-behaviour-tips.

Mischel, Walter; Ebbesen, Ebbe B. (1970). *Attention in Delay of Gratification*. Journal of Personality and Social Psychology. 16 (2): 329–337. doi:10.1037/h0029815. ISSN 0022-3514. S2CID 53464175.

Sachs, D. (1973). *On Freud's Doctrine of Emotions*. Social Research, 40(2), 229-247. Retrieved March 24, 2021, from http://www.jstor.org/stable/40970137

Bhandari, S. (2019). **Nonstimulants and other ADHD drugs**. WebMD. https://www.webmd.com/add-adhd/adhd-nonstimulant-drugs-therapy

CDC. (2021). **Data and statistics about ADHD.** Centers for Disease Control and Prevention. https://www.cdc.gov/ncbddd/adhd/data.html CDC. (2021). **Data and statistics about ADHD.** Centers for Disease Control and Prevention. https://www.cdc.gov/ncbddd/adhd/data.html CHADD. (2021). **ADHD and long-term outcomes**. https://chadd.org/about-adhd/long-term-outcomes/.

CHADD. (2021). **Tics and tourette syndrome.** https://chadd.org/about-adhd/tics-and-tourette-syndrome.

Cram. (2021). **Behavior therapy by B. F. Skinner›s goals and methods**. Cram.com. https://www.cram.com/essay/Behavior-Therapy-By-B-F-Skinners-Goals/F3SSNJ5KGZKQ.

Faraone, S. and Larsson, H. (2019). Genetics of attention deficit hyperactivity disorder. Molecular Psychiatry, 24, pp.562–575.

Hallowell, E. and Jensen, P. (2021). **The ADHD soul shine kit: Build your child's self esteem.** ADDitude. https://www.additudemag.com/self-esteem-build-adhd-child-confidence/

Healthline. (2020). **14 signs of ADHD: Does your child have ADHD?.** Healthline. https://www.healthline.com/health/adhd/signs#lack-of-focus.

Healthline. (2021). **What's bipolar disorder? How do I know if I have it?.** Healthline. https://www.healthline.com/health/bipolar-disorder Healthline. (2021). **Why having ADHD can be a benefit**. Healthline. https://www.healthline.com/health/adhd/benefits-of-adhd.

Kessler, E. (2021). **Dr. Amen's 7 types of ADHD**. Smart Kids. https://www.smartkidswithld.org/getting-help/adhd/7-types-adhd/.

Mayo Clinic. (2021). **Oppositional defiant disorder (ODD) - Symptoms and causes**. https://www.mayoclinic.org/diseases-conditions/oppositional-defiant-disorder/symptoms-causes/syc-20375831

NHS. (2021). **Attention deficit hyperactivity disorder ADHD**. https://www.nhs.uk/conditions/attention-deficit-hyperactivity-disorder-adh Ochoa, J. (2016). Free webinar replay: **Emotional distress syndrome and the ADHD brain.** ADDitude. https://www.additudemag.com/webinar/emotional-distress-syndrome-adhd-brain/

Ratini, M. (2020). **Tic disorders and twitches.** WebMD. https://www.webmd.com/brain/tic-disorders-and_twitches Robinson, L., Smith, M., A, M., Segal, J. and Ramsey, D. (2020). **ADHD medications - HelpGuide.org.** HelpGuide.org. https://www.helpguide.org/articles/add-adhd/medication-for-attention-deficit-disorder-adhd.htm#

Silver, L. (2019). **ADHD medication side effects no one should tolerate.** ADDitude. https://www.additudemag.com/adhd-medication-side-effects-that-no-one-should-tolerate/.

Singer, E. (2007). A neurological basis for ADHD. **MIT Technology Review.** https://www.technologyreview.com/2007/08/09/224410/a-neurological-basis-for-adhd**.**

Usami, M. (2016). Functional consequences of attention-deficit hyperactivity disorder on children and their families. Psychiatry and Clinical Neurosciences, 70(8), pp.303-317.

Hatfield, H. (2021, March 12). 8 Tips for talking to your child about ADHD. *WebMD.* https://www.webmd.com/add-adhd/childhood-adhd/features/adhd-talking-to-child.

Holland, K. (2020, March 25). Celebrities with ADHD: 9 Famous people with ADHD. *Healthline*. https://www.healthline.com/health/adhd/celebrities.

Legg, T. (2020, February 19). *14 Signs of ADHD: does your child have ADHD?* Healthline. https://www.healthline.com/health/adhd/signs.

Schreier, J. (2020, February 24). *Helping a child with ADHD develop social skills*. Mayo Clinic Health System. https://www.mayoclinichealthsystem.org/hometown-health/speaking-of-health/helping-a-child-with-adhd-develop-social-skills.

U.S. Department of Health and Human Services. (n.d.). *Brain basics: The life and death of a neuron*. National Institute of Neurological Disorders and Stroke. https://www.ninds.nih.gov/Disorders/Patient-Caregiver-Education/Life-and-Death-Neuron#:~:text=There%20are%20three%20classes%20of,other%20neurons%20are%20called%20interneurons.

Rachael E. Jack, Oliver G.B. Garrod, Philippe G. Schyns. Dynamic Facial Expressions of Emotion Transmit an Evolving Hierarchy of Signals over Time. Current Biology, 2014; 24 (2): 187 DOI: 10.1016/j.cub.2013.11.064

The vector from www.freepik.com (Commercial License)

Manufactured by Amazon.ca
Acheson, AB